Small-Scale Industries

Small-Scale Industries

Local Economies Backbone

Mack Rafeal

UNIEK ENTERPRISES

CONTENTS

INDEX

Chapter 1

Introduction

In the unpredictable embroidered artwork of the worldwide economy, limited scope enterprises frequently slip through the cracks or eclipsed by their bigger partners. However, these unobtrusive, honest endeavors structure the foundation of nearby economies across the world. Limited scope enterprises are the unrecognized yet truly great individuals of monetary turn of events, cultivating flexibility, advancement, and local area attachment. In this far reaching presentation, we will investigate the meaning of limited scope ventures, their parts in supporting neighborhood economies, and the difficulties they face in an always changing worldwide scene.

Limited scope ventures, frequently alluded to as house businesses or miniature endeavors, include an immense range of organizations. These undertakings are portrayed by their restricted size of tasks, unassuming labor force, and frequently basic creation processes. They act as the help of endless neighborhood networks, adding to monetary development, destitution decrease, and the general prosperity of the populace.

The foundation of neighborhood economies, limited scope enterprises, assume a diverse part in the public eye. They, most importantly, give work valuable open doors to a critical piece of the populace, particularly in rustic regions where elective wellsprings of business might be restricted. The openness of these positions frequently engages minimized networks, empowering them to get away from the grip of destitution and reliance.

Besides, limited scope ventures show a momentous capacity to advance fair dissemination of riches. Dissimilar to enormous combinations, which might pack abundance in the possession of a couple, limited scope businesses will generally scatter monetary benefits inside the local area. The pay produced from these endeavors straightforwardly helps neighborhood laborers and business visionaries, permitting them to put resources into schooling, medical care, and other fundamental administrations, at last prompting a better of life.

Limited scope businesses additionally reinforce local area flexibility by broadening nearby economies. A district dependent on a solitary huge partnership is helpless against monetary shocks in the event that that company faces monetary hardships or chooses to move. Interestingly, people group with an organization of limited scope endeavors are better prepared to endure monetary choppiness. Their variety guarantees that regardless of whether one business wavers, others can step in to fill the hole.

The idea of limited scope businesses rises above boundaries and societies. These undertakings have demonstrated to be a worldwide peculiarity, supporting economies in created and emerging countries the same.

In industrialized nations, limited scope ventures have advanced as powerful players in specialty markets, frequently succeeding in areas of development and craftsmanship. Interestingly, non-industrial countries depend vigorously on limited scope enterprises to overcome any issues among formal and casual areas, giving a crucial method for money for a huge part of the populace.

One of the characterizing elements of limited scope ventures is their flexibility. They display the momentous capacity to develop and take special care of changing customer inclinations and market requests. Their spryness permits them to answer quickly to shifts in the financial scene, making them appropriate to the difficulties of the advanced period. While enormous enterprises might confront obstacles in rebuilding their tasks to oblige new advances and market patterns, limited scope businesses can turn effortlessly.

Limited scope businesses are additionally instrumental in advancing practical financial turn of events. Their nearness to nearby networks implies that they frequently have a personal stake in protecting the climate and guaranteeing the prosperity of the area. Not at all like enormous, global organizations, limited scope enterprises as often as possible do whatever it may take to limit their natural effect and put resources into feasible practices.

The job of limited scope businesses in animating advancement ought to be considered carefully. These undertakings are in many cases centers of imagination and trial and error. Nearby craftsmans, craftspeople, and makers regularly saddle their personal information on the local area's requirements and inclinations to deliver novel, attractive labor and products. This limited way to deal with advancement can prompt the improvement of items that are more custom-made to the neighborhood culture and climate.

Besides, limited scope enterprises can cultivate a feeling of local area and social safeguarding. In an undeniably globalized world, these undertakings act as stores of custom and neighborhood personality. They produce labor and products that mirror the one of a kind qualities and legacy of their networks, frequently assuming a crucial part in keeping social practices alive.

Nonetheless, regardless of their significant commitments, limited scope enterprises are not without their difficulties. In numerous locales, these ventures face a scope of hindrances that compromise their maintainability. One of the most major problems is admittance to capital. Restricted monetary assets can upset the development and extension of limited scope businesses. Numerous business people battle to get advances or ventures, which can smother development and extension.

Also, limited scope businesses frequently wrestle with deficient framework, including restricted admittance to dependable power, transportation, and correspondence organizations. These inadequacies can increment creation costs and confine market reach, making it more challenging for these ventures to contend for a bigger scope.

Administrative weights can likewise represent a huge test for limited scope ventures. Unreasonable administrative noise, complex allowing processes, and burdensome tax assessment can be overpowering for entrepreneurs, redirecting assets from useful exercises and into regulatory obstacles. At times, these guidelines can prompt casualness, as business visionaries decide to work under the table to stay away from the intricacies and expenses of consistence.

The worldwide commercial center, described by wild contest and innovative headways, presents one more test to limited scope businesses. In a climate where economies of scale frequently decide achievement, these organizations might battle to stay up with bigger companies. The absence of assets for innovative work can upset their capacity to take on present day advances, computerize processes, and contend actually.

In spite of these difficulties, limited scope businesses have shown wonderful flexibility, and there is developing acknowledgment of the need to help and enable them. States and global associations are progressively pushing for approaches that work with the development of limited scope businesses, perceiving their capability to drive financial development, lessen neediness, and cultivate nearby turn of events.

1.1 Defining Small-Scale Industries

Limited scope ventures, frequently alluded to as miniature undertakings, cabin enterprises, or just independent companies, envelop a different scope of financial exercises. While there is no all around acknowledged definition, these endeavors share normal attributes that recognize them from bigger organizations and combinations. By and large, limited scope enterprises are described by their restricted size of activities, unassuming labor force, and frequently straightforward creation processes. These organizations commonly have a more modest actual impression, with less framework and hardware contrasted with their bigger partners.

The meaning of limited scope ventures fluctuates starting with one country then onto the next and, surprisingly, inside various businesses. In numerous nations, states and administrative bodies characterize these endeavors in view of variables, for example, the quantity of workers, how much capital contributed, or the degree of creation. For instance, in India, limited scope enterprises are classified in light of their interest in plant and apparatus, while in the US, the Private venture Organization (SBA) utilizes representative count and income to order private ventures.

In India, for example, miniature undertakings are characterized as those with interests in plant and apparatus up to INR 25 lakhs (around $33,000). Limited scope enterprises, then again, are characterized as those with ventures between INR 25 lakhs and INR 5 crores (around \$33,000 to \$670,000). This grouping is utilized to benefit different government impetuses and strategies custom fitted to help these endeavors. Essentially, the European Association has an alternate arrangement of models, taking into account factors like the quantity of workers, yearly turnover, and fiscal summaries to characterize little and medium-sized endeavors (SMEs).

No matter what the particular boundaries utilized for arrangement, limited scope businesses assume an irreplaceable part in nearby economies, and their commitments reach out a long ways past the numbers that characterize them. These organizations are the overlooked yet truly great individuals of monetary turn of events, and their importance couldn't possibly be more significant. They are much of the time the essential wellspring of work in numerous districts, especially in country regions where bigger organizations might be missing.

Limited scope businesses have an intrinsic capacity to enable underestimated networks by giving available open positions. This is particularly crucial in emerging nations, where joblessness and underemployment can be major problems. By offering work to nearby occupants, these endeavors assist with decreasing destitution and reliance, further developing the general prosperity of the populace.

Moreover, limited scope ventures add to impartial abundance circulation. Not at all like enormous enterprises that might pack abundance in the possession of a limited handful investors, limited scope ventures frequently scatter monetary benefits inside the local area. The pay produced from these ventures straightforwardly helps nearby laborers and business visionaries, permitting them to put resources into training, medical care, and other fundamental administrations, eventually prompting an improvement in their personal satisfaction.

The presence of limited scope ventures likewise encourages local area strength. Rather than locales excessively dependent on a solitary huge partnership, networks with an organization of limited scope ventures are better prepared to endure monetary shocks. The variety of these organizations guarantees that, regardless of whether one wavers, others can step in to fill the hole, forestalling disastrous financial slumps locally.

Limited scope enterprises are flexible substances that have been perceived for their versatility. They show an uncanny capacity to develop and take special care of changing buyer inclinations and market requests. Their agility permits them to answer rapidly to shifts in the monetary scene, making them appropriate to the difficulties of the cutting edge period. While enormous enterprises might experience obstacles in rebuilding their tasks to oblige new advancements and market patterns, limited scope businesses can turn effortlessly.

These undertakings likewise assume a huge part in advancing feasible financial turn of events. Their vicinity to nearby networks implies that they frequently have a personal stake in safeguarding the climate and guaranteeing the prosperity of the area. Dissimilar to huge, global organizations, limited scope enterprises oftentimes do whatever it may take to limit their ecological effect and put resources into feasible practices.

Notwithstanding their maintainability endeavors, limited scope enterprises can be centers of development. Neighborhood craftsmans, craftspeople, and makers frequently saddle their close information on the local area's necessities and inclinations to deliver one of a kind, attractive labor and products. This limited way to deal with advancement can prompt the improvement of items that are more customized to the nearby culture and climate.

Limited scope enterprises likewise add to social protection. In an undeniably globalized world, these endeavors act as vaults of custom and nearby character. They produce labor and products that mirror the extraordinary qualities and legacy of their networks, frequently assuming a crucial part in keeping social practices alive.

In any case, in spite of their important commitments, limited scope businesses are not without their difficulties. One of the most major problems is admittance to capital. Restricted monetary assets can block the development and extension of these endeavors. Numerous business people battle to get credits or ventures, which can smother advancement and extension. The absence of admittance to capital additionally restricts their capacity to put resources into innovative work, impeding their seriousness.

Limited scope businesses frequently wrestle with insufficient foundation, including restricted admittance to solid power, transportation, and correspondence organizations. These inadequacies can increment creation costs and confine market reach, making it more hard for these endeavors to contend for a bigger scope. In districts where framework is deficient with regards to, the expense of carrying on with work can be fundamentally higher for limited scope enterprises.

Administrative weights address one more huge test for limited scope enterprises. Inordinate administrative noise, complex allowing processes, and cumbersome tax collection can be overpowering for entrepreneurs, redirecting assets from useful exercises and into regulatory obstacles. Now and again, these guidelines can prompt familiarity, as business visionaries decide to work under the table to keep away from the intricacies and expenses of consistence.

The worldwide commercial center, portrayed by savage rivalry and innovative progressions, presents one more test to limited scope businesses. In a climate where economies of scale frequently decide achievement, these organizations might battle to stay up with bigger enterprises. The absence of assets for innovative work can block their capacity to take on current advances, robotize processes, and contend actually.

Notwithstanding these difficulties, limited scope ventures have shown astounding flexibility, and there is developing acknowledgment of the need to help and engage them. States and global associations are progressively upholding for strategies that work with the development of limited scope ventures, perceiving their capability to drive financial development, decrease neediness, and cultivate nearby turn of events.

Taking everything into account, limited scope businesses are the unrecognized yet truly great individuals of neighborhood economies across the globe. They give business potential open doors, advance evenhanded abundance appropriation, upgrade local area strength, and backing reasonable turn of events. These undertakings are not just the financial spine of their individual locales yet in addition heroes of development, social conservation, and local area personality. The limited scale businesses area is a demonstration of the strength, genius, and getting through soul of neighborhood networks, and it merits the acknowledgment and backing important to keep flourishing in a steadily impacting world. Notwithstanding their humble size, these organizations are obviously strong motors of nearby turn of events and worldwide monetary advancement.

1.2 The Significance of Local Economies

Neighborhood economies are the complicated, interconnected frameworks that shape the social and monetary texture of networks, towns, and locales across the world. They assume a crucial part in encouraging financial turn of events, guaranteeing social union, and adding to the general prosperity of the populace. Neighborhood economies are not segregated substances but instead vital parts of the more extensive public and worldwide financial scene, frequently described by special highlights that recognize them from each other.

The meaning of nearby economies is multi-layered. They act as the establishment whereupon public and worldwide economies are fabricated. They address the substance of financial versatility, maintainability, and flexibility, and their wellbeing straightforwardly influences the success of a country. Neighborhood economies are the favorable places for business, development, and social protection, making them fundamental parts of a country's social and financial character.

At the core of any nearby economy are the organizations that work inside it. These organizations can go from limited scope businesses and mother and-pop stores to bigger ventures with provincial importance. Specifically, limited scope ventures, frequently the foundation of nearby economies, are basic in producing work open doors and guaranteeing that monetary assets course inside the local area.

Neighborhood organizations are fundamental for giving position to the nearby labor force, and this work frequently reaches out to the minimized and weak sections of the populace. Limited scope enterprises, specifically, assume a vital part in such manner. Their availability and more modest labor force necessities make them key supporters of lessening joblessness and neediness, particularly in provincial regions where elective wellsprings of business might be scant.

Besides, neighborhood organizations contribute fundamentally to evenhanded abundance appropriation. They tend to reinvest their income into the neighborhood local area by recruiting nearby specialists and obtaining nearby labor and products.

This monetary course has a multiplier impact, as it brings about expanded spending and, eventually, worked on expectations for everyday comforts inside the locale.

Local area versatility is one more basic feature of the meaning of neighborhood economies. Networks with expanded nearby economies are more ready to climate financial shocks, whether welcomed on by changes in purchaser inclinations, vacillations in market interest, or worldwide monetary emergencies. Conversely, people group intensely subject to a solitary industry or boss might be especially defenseless against financial slumps when that industry flounders.

Nearby economies, with their characteristic connect to their environmental factors, have a personal stake in saving the climate and guaranteeing the general prosperity of the area. These economies frequently focus on supportable practices, both out of ecological obligation and for long haul practicality. Limited scope businesses, specifically, are bound to take on eco-accommodating creation techniques and backing nearby drives that advance manageability.

Besides, neighborhood economies act as pots of advancement. They give a fruitful ground to business visionaries and trend-setters to foster new items and administrations that are custom fitted to the one of a kind requirements and inclinations of the local area. Limited scope enterprises, driven by their vicinity to neighborhood customers, much of the time outfit their insight to deliver products that mirror the way of life and legacy of their district, adding to a feeling of nearby personality.

Social safeguarding is one more part of the meaning of nearby economies. In an undeniably globalized world, these economies frequently champion conventional specialties, artistic expressions, and social practices. They are fundamental for shielding and sending the exceptional social legacy of a locale, in this manner adding to its character and history.

While nearby economies assume a urgent part in supporting the government assistance and dynamic quality of their networks, they are not resistant to challenges. A few variables can upset their supportability and development. One of the most major problems is the opposition and impact of bigger partnerships. Worldwide combinations frequently have the assets to enter and rule nearby business sectors, pressing out more modest organizations and adjusting the elements of neighborhood economies.

Admittance to capital is one more huge test for nearby organizations, particularly limited scope ventures. Restricted monetary assets can block their development and extension. Business people frequently battle to get credits or speculations, which can smother advancement and development. This absence of admittance to capital additionally restricts their capacity to put resources into innovative work, preventing their intensity.

Deficient foundation can likewise represent a critical boundary for nearby economics. Numerous areas miss the mark on components, for example, dependable power, transportation organizations, and correspondence frameworks.

This inadequacy can prompt expanded creation costs and confined market reach, making it more hard for nearby organizations to contend for a bigger scope.

Administrative difficulties are one more major problem for nearby organizations. Extreme organization, complex allowing processes, and oppressive tax collection can be overpowering for entrepreneurs, redirecting assets from useful exercises and into managerial obstacles. At times, these guidelines can prompt familiarity, as business visionaries decide to work under the table to keep away from the intricacies and expenses of consistence.

Globalization presents its own arrangement of difficulties for neighborhood economies. The worldwide commercial center, set apart by furious contest and mechanical headways, can be an impressive enemy for limited scope enterprises. In a climate where economies of scale frequently decide achievement, these organizations might battle to stay up with bigger companies. The absence of assets for innovative work can thwart their capacity to embrace current advancements, mechanize processes, and contend successfully.

Regardless of these difficulties, nearby economies have shown momentous flexibility, and there is developing acknowledgment of the need to help and enable them. States, nearby specialists, and global associations are progressively pushing for arrangements that work with the development of neighborhood economies, perceiving their capability to drive monetary development, lessen neediness, and encourage nearby turn of events.

Taking everything into account, nearby economies are the soul of networks all over the planet. They are fundamental for giving business, guaranteeing fair abundance dispersion, cultivating local area strength, and supporting reasonable turn of events. Neighborhood economies are not just about deals; they are likewise about the social character and legacy of a locale. These economies are necessary to the prosperity and success of individuals living in these networks, and their importance couldn't possibly be more significant. The difficulties they face are genuine, however with the right help and procedures, nearby economies can flourish and keep on being the motors of neighborhood advancement and worldwide monetary advancement.

1.3 Purpose and Scope of the Book

This book is a far reaching investigation of a diverse and indispensable subject — limited scope businesses and their job as the foundation of nearby economies. Inside these pages, we mean to reveal insight into the central attributes, importance, difficulties, and capability of limited scope businesses, inspecting how they add to the dynamic quality and strength of neighborhood economies. This work tries to act as an aide, a wellspring of information, and a stage for conversation, offering bits of knowledge and data to policymakers, business visionaries, scholastics, and anyone with any interest at all in getting it and cultivating the development of limited scope ventures in the cutting edge world.

At its center, the reason for this book is to offer a more profound comprehension of limited scope ventures and their significant effect on neighborhood economies. We look to disentangle the complexities of these endeavors, demystify their commitments, and reveal the difficulties they face. Thusly, we expect to feature their importance and potential, and to add to the continuous talk on financial turn of events, work age, development, and local area manageability.

In this investigation, we will dive into the actual pith of limited scope ventures. We will inspect their main traits, which incorporate restricted size of activities, unobtrusive labor force, and frequently basic creation processes. We will talk about the assorted structures they take, from neighborhood creates and high quality creation to particular assembling and administrations. All through the book, we will grandstand the flexibility and versatility of limited scope enterprises, representing how they can develop, advance, and stay significant in a steadily changing worldwide scene.

The extent of this book is immense, incorporating a great many subjects connected with limited scope ventures and neighborhood economies. We will break down their commitments to work age, evenhanded abundance circulation, local area versatility, and reasonable turn of events. We will investigate the manners by which limited scope businesses advance development, social protection, and a feeling of neighborhood personality. We will likewise examine the difficulties they face, from admittance to capital and deficient framework to administrative weights and the opposition presented by bigger organizations.

All through this extensive investigation, we will give certifiable models, contextual analyses, and information driven bits of knowledge to help our contentions and show the variety of limited scope ventures around the world. We will likewise draw from existing examination, well-qualified suppositions, and the encounters of business people and policymakers to offer a balanced point of view regarding the matter.

One of the key perspectives we expect to address in this book is the approach scene encompassing limited scope businesses. State run administrations and global associations are progressively perceiving the significance of these undertakings and executing approaches to help their development and maintainability. We will look at these approaches, taking into account their effect and adequacy, and talk about likely areas of progress. We want to give an asset that can illuminate and direct policymakers in creating systems to enable limited scope businesses and, likewise, nearby economies.

One more fundamental component of the book is the job of business with regards to limited scope enterprises. We will investigate the attitude, abilities, and difficulties that business visionaries face while setting out on limited scope adventures. We will examine the meaning of business in driving advancement and monetary turn of events, and how it tends to be sustained and empowered in different districts.

Besides, we will look at the job of innovation and digitalization in the development of limited scope businesses. The computerized age has carried the two potential open doors and difficulties to these undertakings. We will survey the manners by which innovation can upgrade their seriousness and market reach, as well as the advanced gap that might abandon a few limited scope ventures.

While our essential spotlight is on limited scope ventures in emerging countries, we will likewise address the elements of these undertakings in created nations. We will investigate how limited scope ventures have advanced to succeed in specialty markets, driven by development and craftsmanship, and how they keep on flourishing even with globalization and large scale manufacturing.

The meaning of this book stretches out past scholarly community. It means to give reasonable bits of knowledge and proposals to business visionaries hoping to lay out or grow limited scope ventures, offering direction on the most proficient method to defeat difficulties and expand their true capacity. It likewise fills in as an important asset for policymakers trying to establish an empowering climate for the development of limited scope businesses.

As the world countenances monetary difficulties, the aftermath of worldwide pandemics, and the requirement for manageable turn of events, limited scope enterprises play an essential part to play. They are not only curious leftovers of the past; they are dynamic, strong, and vital parts of the advanced economy. This book tries to enable perusers with the information and understanding important to tackle the capability of limited scope ventures, adding to the success and manageability of neighborhood economies all over the planet.

Taking everything into account, the reason and extent of this book are aggressive, mirroring the current intricacy and meaning of the subject. Limited scope enterprises and neighborhood economies are complicatedly interwoven, and their investigation requires a complex point of view. We welcome perusers to leave on this excursion with us, as we disentangle the different features of limited scope ventures, from their commitments to difficulties and potential, offering experiences that can illuminate strategies, motivate business visionaries, and add to the continuous talk on the foundation of nearby economies.

Chapter 2

Small-Scale Industries and Economic Growth

Limited scope enterprises, frequently eclipsed by their bigger partners, hold a special and crucial spot in the more extensive scene of monetary development. While global partnerships and aggregates order significant consideration and assets, the limited scale businesses are in many cases the uncelebrated yet truly great individuals of nearby and territorial monetary turn of events. Their commitments to monetary development are complex and significant, making them a principal driver of flourishing, work, and flexibility in numerous economies.

At the core of understanding the connection between limited scope businesses and monetary development is perceiving the assorted and dynamic nature of these undertakings. They are ordinarily portrayed by their restricted size of tasks, unobtrusive labor force, and frequently basic creation processes. These organizations can incorporate a huge swath of areas, going from customary distinctive specialties to particular assembling and a wide assortment of administrations. This variety loans them their exceptional and crucial job in driving financial development.

One of the main commitments of limited scope businesses to financial development is their ability to create work potential open doors. These ventures, by uprightness of their more modest size and decentralized nature, are much of the time profoundly implanted inside neighborhood networks. They give available open positions, particularly in districts where elective wellsprings of work might be scant. The significance of this job couldn't possibly be more significant, especially in country regions and emerging nations, where joblessness and underemployment can be intense issues.

The openness of work in limited scope ventures enables minimized networks and people who might have restricted admittance to formal work markets. By extending to nearby employment opportunities, these undertakings can essentially diminish neediness and reliance, work on expectations for everyday comforts, and upgrade the general prosperity of the populace. They likewise assume a part in orientation uniformity, as they frequently give open doors to ladies to take part in the labor force, advancing monetary freedom and strengthening.

Evenhanded abundance appropriation is one more urgent part of the commitment of limited scope ventures to monetary development. Dissimilar to enormous organizations, which can move abundance in the possession of a chosen handful investors, limited scope ventures will generally scatter monetary profits inside the local area.

The pay produced from these ventures straightforwardly helps nearby specialists and business people, permitting them to put resources into training, medical care, and other fundamental administrations. This reallocation of abundance inside the local area encourages social and monetary inclusivity, lessening pay abberations and improving in general flourishing.

Limited scope businesses likewise encourage local area versatility, a basic consider supporting monetary development. Rather than locales intensely dependent on a solitary industry or boss, networks with an organization of limited scope ventures are better prepared to endure financial shocks. The variety of these organizations guarantees that, regardless of whether one flounders, others can step in to fill the hole. This strength is especially obvious in the midst of financial emergencies, like the new worldwide pandemic, where limited scope businesses have frequently shown striking flexibility and development.

The versatility and adaptability of limited scope ventures are key components that add to monetary development. These ventures show an uncanny capacity to turn and answer quickly to changes in the monetary scene. While enormous companies might confront obstacles in rebuilding their tasks to oblige new advancements and market patterns, limited scope businesses can move their concentration effortlessly. This flexibility permits them to quickly jump all over arising chances, answer developing customer inclinations, and stay serious in a quickly impacting world.

Limited scope businesses have likewise exhibited their ability to advance practical monetary development. Their nearness to neighborhood networks implies that they frequently have a personal stake in saving the climate and guaranteeing the prosperity of the area. Not at all like enormous, worldwide enterprises, limited scope ventures often do whatever it takes to limit their natural effect and put resources into manageable practices. This obligation to maintainability lines up with the developing worldwide accentuation on dependable and eco-accommodating strategic policies, making limited scope enterprises significant supporters of green and moral monetary development.

Moreover, limited scope ventures are instrumental in driving development, a crucial driver of monetary development in the cutting edge world. Nearby craftsmans, craftspeople, and makers frequently saddle their close information on the local area's necessities and inclinations to deliver remarkable, attractive labor and products. This restricted way to deal with advancement can prompt the improvement of items that are more custom-made to the nearby culture and climate. It likewise cultivates a culture of inventiveness and trial and error that can prompt the revelation of new, attractive thoughts.

Social safeguarding is one more element of the effect of limited scope ventures on monetary development. In an undeniably globalized world, these ventures act as stores of custom and neighborhood personality.

They produce labor and products that mirror the extraordinary qualities and legacy of their networks, frequently assuming a crucial part in keeping social practices alive. By supporting nearby craftsmanship and social practices, limited scope enterprises add to the protection of a district's character and history.

Be that as it may, in spite of their priceless commitments, limited scope businesses are not without their difficulties. Perhaps of the most major problem they face is admittance to capital. Restricted monetary assets can thwart the development and extension of these ventures. Numerous business people battle to get credits or speculations, which can smother advancement and extension. The absence of admittance to capital additionally restricts their capacity to put resources into innovative work, upsetting their intensity and capacity to quickly jump all over development chances.

Insufficient framework, including restricted admittance to dependable power, transportation, and correspondence organizations, is one more critical test for limited scope enterprises. These inadequacies can increment creation costs and confine market reach, making it more hard for these undertakings to contend for a bigger scope. Admittance to framework is many times a basic figure deciding the intensity and development capability of limited scope businesses.

Administrative weights address one more significant test for limited scope businesses. Inordinate administrative noise, complex allowing processes, and grave tax collection can be overpowering for entrepreneurs, redirecting assets from useful exercises and into regulatory obstacles. At times, these guidelines can prompt casualness, as business people decide to work under the table to stay away from the intricacies and expenses of consistence. Administrative change and disentanglement are urgent for improving the development possibilities of limited scope enterprises.

The worldwide commercial center, described by furious contest and innovative headways, presents a critical test to limited scope enterprises. In a climate where economies of scale frequently decide achievement, these organizations might battle to stay up with bigger partnerships. The absence of assets for innovative work can block their capacity to embrace current advancements, computerize processes, and contend actually. To flourish in the worldwide economy, limited scope businesses need procedures that permit them to use their one of a kind qualities while tending to their limits.

The Coronavirus pandemic, a worldwide emergency with significant financial results, has highlighted the significance of nearby economies and limited scope enterprises. Numerous people group have gone to these undertakings as wellsprings of fundamental labor and products during the pandemic, featuring their basic job in guaranteeing the versatility and prosperity of nearby populaces. Nonetheless, the pandemic has likewise introduced difficulties, including production network interruptions, diminished buyer spending, and the requirement for new security measures.

Limited scope businesses that have adjusted rapidly to these difficulties have exhibited their deftness and versatility.

2.1 The Economic Contribution of Small Businesses

Independent ventures are the unrecognized yet truly great individuals of economies around the world. While global organizations and enormous endeavors frequently snatch the titles, the private companies assume an essential and multi-layered part in driving financial development, work creation, development, and local area prosperity. Their importance goes past their sheer number; they are the foundation of numerous economies, contributing in assorted and significant ways. In this extensive investigation, we dig into the financial commitment of private companies, revealing insight into their significance and effect on neighborhood and public economies.

Private companies, frequently portrayed by their restricted size of tasks, unassuming labor force, and pioneering soul, come in different structures, from mother and-pop shops and neighborhood distinctive specialties to specific specialist organizations. These ventures are profoundly incorporated into their networks, taking care of nearby necessities and requests. Their tasks, while little in scale, cover a wide range of areas, going from retail and assembling to innovation, proficient administrations, and imaginative ventures.

One of the most essential commitments of private ventures to the economy is their job in work age. They are motors of occupation creation, utilizing a huge part of the labor force in numerous districts. The openness of work valuable open doors given by private ventures is many times a help for neighborhood occupants, especially in regions where bigger companies might be missing. These organizations act as essential wellsprings of business, assisting with lessening joblessness and underemployment, which are normal difficulties, particularly in agricultural nations.

Private ventures likewise advance evenhanded abundance dispersion inside networks. In contrast to huge organizations, where benefits will generally gather in the possession of a couple of investors, private companies frequently reinvest their profit locally. The pay produced from these undertakings straightforwardly helps the neighborhood labor force, as well as the business people who began the organizations. This monetary flow animates financial action inside the local area, prompting expanded spending and generally speaking superior expectations for everyday comforts.

Moreover, the monetary versatility of networks is frequently intently attached to the presence of private ventures. Locales vigorously dependent on a solitary industry or boss can be especially helpless against monetary shocks. Conversely, people group with a different biological system of private companies are better prepared to climate monetary slumps. That's what the variety guarantees, regardless of whether one business vacillates, others can step in to fill the hole, forestalling devastating financial decreases locally.

Independent ventures are famous for their deftness and versatility. They can answer quickly to changes in economic situations, customer inclinations, and financial patterns. This adaptability makes them appropriate to the difficulties of the cutting edge time. Not at all like huge organizations, which might confront obstacles in rebuilding their activities to oblige new advancements and market elements, private ventures can turn no sweat.

Supportability is one more component of the financial commitment of independent ventures. Their closeness to neighborhood networks frequently prompts a personal stake in saving the climate and guaranteeing the prosperity of the area. Private ventures oftentimes embrace feasible practices, like diminishing waste, monitoring assets, and supporting nearby drives for natural assurance. This obligation to supportability lines up with the developing accentuation on green and moral strategic policies, making independent companies fundamental supporters of capable financial development.

Independent ventures are likewise centers of advancement and imagination. Business people and entrepreneurs frequently have a cozy information on their networks' necessities and inclinations, permitting them to foster remarkable items and administrations. This confined way to deal with development prompts the production of merchandise and arrangements that are more custom fitted to the neighborhood culture and climate. It encourages a culture of trial and error, critical thinking, and variation, which can prompt the revelation of new, attractive thoughts.

Social conservation is one more component of the monetary commitment of private ventures. In an undeniably globalized world, these ventures act as gatekeepers of custom and nearby personality. They produce labor and products that mirror the extraordinary qualities and legacy of their networks, frequently assuming a crucial part in saving social customs and practices. By supporting nearby craftsmanship and social exercises, private companies add to the conservation of a locale's personality and history.

Private ventures are not without their difficulties. Admittance to capital is a critical obstacle for some business visionaries. Restricted monetary assets can prevent the development and extension of these endeavors. Numerous entrepreneurs battle to get credits or speculations, which can smother development and extension. The absence of admittance to capital additionally restricts their capacity to put resources into innovative work, hampering their seriousness and capacity to immediately take advantage of development chances.

Insufficient foundation, including restricted admittance to dependable power, transportation, and correspondence organizations, can likewise represent a critical obstruction for private ventures. These inadequacies can increment creation costs and confine market reach, making it more hard for these undertakings to contend for a bigger scope. Admittance to current foundation is many times a basic figure deciding the intensity and development capability of private ventures.

Administrative weights address one more huge test for private companies. Extreme organization, complex allowing processes, and burdensome tax collection can be overpowering for entrepreneurs, redirecting assets from useful exercises and into managerial obstacles. Now and again, these guidelines can prompt casualness, as business visionaries decide to work under the table to keep away from the intricacies and expenses of consistence. Administrative change and rearrangements are essential for improving the development possibilities of private companies.

The worldwide commercial center, described by savage contest and mechanical headways, presents a significant test to independent companies. In a climate where economies of scale frequently decide achievement, these organizations might battle to stay up with bigger partnerships. The absence of assets for innovative work can prevent their capacity to embrace current advancements, computerize processes, and contend actually. To flourish in the worldwide economy, private companies need systems that permit them to use their one of a kind qualities while tending to their limits.

The Coronavirus pandemic has put remarkable weight on independent ventures around the world. Many have confronted difficulties, for example, store network disturbances, diminished purchaser spending, and the need to adjust to new security measures. By the by, private ventures have exhibited versatility, flexibility, and a solid feeling of local area during the emergency. They have been instrumental in giving fundamental labor and products during the pandemic, highlighting their significance to neighborhood networks.

All in all, private companies are not simple references in the monetary scene; they are the backbone of neighborhood and public economies. Their financial commitments stretch out past work creation and impartial abundance circulation. They are drivers of development, manageability, and social conservation. While they face difficulties connected with admittance to capital, framework, guidelines, and rivalry from bigger partnerships, their importance in nearby and worldwide economies couldn't possibly be more significant. Engaging and supporting private ventures isn't just a question of financial development yet in addition a method for protecting social legacy, advance maintainability, and guarantee the prosperity of nearby networks. Private ventures are fundamental accomplices in the mission for comprehensive and capable monetary development.

2.2 Local Employment and Income Generation

Nearby work and pay age are at the core of flourishing networks and economies. In the many-sided trap of worldwide monetary frameworks, nearby economies assume an essential part in guaranteeing that people approach livelihoods and that monetary assets course inside the local area. While enormous partnerships and worldwide organizations frequently overwhelm the financial scene, the little and nearby organizations act as essential supporters of business and pay age in numerous districts.

In this exhaustive investigation, we dig into the meaning of nearby business and pay age, revealing their diverse effect on networks, people, and the more extensive economy.

Neighborhood business is a foundation of financial prosperity and local area strength. It is through work open doors that people and families access the assets important to meet their essential necessities, accomplish financial security, and put resources into their future. Neighborhood organizations, including little and medium-sized ventures (SMEs), are fundamental for giving position to the nearby labor force. These organizations act as fundamental wellsprings of work, assisting with lessening joblessness and underemployment, which can be especially major problems, particularly in agricultural nations.

The openness of work potential open doors given by neighborhood organizations enables underestimated networks and people who might have restricted admittance to formal work markets. In districts where enormous enterprises are missing or have restricted presence, little and neighborhood organizations assume a basic part in giving open and nearby open positions. This supports neighborhood inhabitants as well as adds to decreased neediness and reliance, at last working on expectations for everyday comforts and improving the general prosperity of the populace.

Nearby work significantly affects orientation uniformity. Little and nearby organizations frequently give potential open doors to ladies to partake in the labor force. In numerous networks, these ventures are instrumental in propelling orientation equity by extending open positions, monetary autonomy, and strengthening to ladies. The meaning of this job in supporting orientation value couldn't possibly be more significant, as it assists separate customary hindrances and standards that with having limited ladies' cooperation in the labor force.

Impartial abundance dissemination is one more key element of neighborhood business and pay age. In contrast to enormous partnerships, where benefits frequently gather in the possession of a chosen handful investors, nearby organizations much of the time reinvest their profit locally. The pay produced from these endeavors straightforwardly helps the neighborhood labor force, as well as the business visionaries and entrepreneurs. This monetary flow invigorates financial action inside the local area, prompting expanded spending and, at last, worked on expectations for everyday comforts.

Local area versatility is characteristically connected to nearby work. Districts vigorously dependent on a solitary industry or manager can be especially defenseless against monetary shocks. Interestingly, people group with a different biological system of nearby organizations are better prepared to endure financial slumps. That's what the variety guarantees, regardless of whether one business faces difficulties, others can step in to fill the hole, forestalling devastating monetary decreases locally. This flexibility is especially obvious in the midst of monetary emergencies, like the new worldwide pandemic, where nearby organizations have frequently shown surprising versatility and advancement.

Neighborhood organizations are known for their versatility and capacity to turn rapidly in light of changes in economic situations, purchaser inclinations, and financial patterns. This flexibility is a basic calculate nearby work and pay age. While huge organizations might confront obstacles in rebuilding their activities to oblige new advances and market elements, nearby organizations can move their concentration no sweat. This adaptability makes them appropriate to the difficulties of the cutting edge time.

Nearby organizations are much of the time inserted inside the texture of their networks. They have a profound comprehension of the neighborhood culture, necessities, and inclinations, which positions them well to give custom fitted labor and products. This restricted way to deal with business fulfills nearby requests as well as encourages a feeling of local area character. It adds to the conservation of customs, culture, and nearby legacy, making a more grounded connection among organizations and their clients.

Social safeguarding is one more element of the effect of nearby work and pay age. In an undeniably globalized world, neighborhood organizations frequently act as watchmen of custom and nearby personality. They produce labor and products that mirror the remarkable qualities and legacy of their networks, frequently assuming a fundamental part in saving social customs and practices. By supporting nearby craftsmanship and social exercises, neighborhood organizations add to the protection of a locale's personality and history.

In any case, in spite of their various commitments, neighborhood organizations and nearby work face difficulties that can upset their development and supportability. One of the main difficulties is admittance to capital. Restricted monetary assets can confine the extension and improvement of these organizations. Numerous business people battle to get advances or speculations, which can smother development and extension. The absence of admittance to capital likewise restricts their capacity to put resources into innovative work, hampering their intensity and capacity to immediately jump all over development chances.

Deficient foundation, including restricted admittance to dependable power, transportation, and correspondence organizations, can likewise represent a huge obstruction for nearby organizations. These lacks can increment creation costs and confine market reach, making it more hard for these endeavors to contend for a bigger scope. Admittance to present day framework is much of the time a basic consider deciding the seriousness and development capability of nearby organizations.

Administrative weights address one more significant test for nearby organizations. Exorbitant organization, complex allowing processes, and grave tax assessment can be overpowering for entrepreneurs, redirecting assets from useful exercises and into regulatory obstacles. At times, these guidelines can prompt casualness, as business visionaries decide to work under the table to keep away from the intricacies and expenses of consistence. Administrative change and rearrangements are critical for upgrading the development possibilities of neighborhood organizations and nearby business.

The worldwide commercial center, set apart by wild contest and innovative headways, presents a huge test for neighborhood organizations. In a climate where economies of scale frequently decide achievement, these organizations might battle to stay up with bigger enterprises. The absence of assets for innovative work can thwart their capacity to take on present day advancements, robotize processes, and contend actually. To flourish in the worldwide economy, neighborhood organizations need methodologies that permit them to use their exceptional assets while tending to their constraints.

The Coronavirus pandemic, a worldwide emergency with significant financial results, has highlighted the significance of neighborhood organizations and nearby work. Numerous people group have gone to these organizations as wellsprings of fundamental labor and products during the pandemic, featuring their basic job in guaranteeing the versatility and prosperity of neighborhood populaces. By the by, the pandemic has introduced difficulties, including production network disturbances, diminished purchaser spending, and the need to adjust to new wellbeing measures. Nearby organizations that have adjusted rapidly to these difficulties have exhibited their spryness and strength.

Taking everything into account, neighborhood business and pay age are fundamental parts of flourishing networks and strong economies. They are not just about positions and monetary assets; they are about prosperity, strengthening, and the safeguarding of culture and character. While challenges connected with admittance to capital, foundation, guidelines, and contest from bigger organizations exist, their importance in neighborhood and worldwide economies couldn't possibly be more significant. Engaging and supporting neighborhood organizations and nearby work isn't just a question of monetary development yet in addition a method for advancing social union, supportability, and local area prosperity. Neighborhood organizations and nearby business are central to the texture of dynamic networks and prosperous economies.

Chapter 3

Entrepreneurship and Innovation

Business and advancement are two mainstays of financial development and progress, driving groundbreaking change and cultivating the dynamism of present day economies. The harmonious connection between these two ideas is basic in reshaping enterprises, presenting novel arrangements, and catalyzing headways in innovation and plans of action. This complete investigation dives into the entwined universe of business venture and advancement, unwinding their significant effect on neighborhood and worldwide economies and the basic job they play in molding what's in store.

Business venture, frequently described by risk-taking and the quest for open doors, is a main thrust behind financial development. Business visionaries are people who distinguish holes or needs on the lookout and make new dares to address them. They are the visionary daring individuals who imagine inventive arrangements and assemble assets to carry them to completion. These business visionaries, whether they work little nearby organizations or send off tech new companies, are the planners of financial advancement.

The meaning of business in monetary development is multi-layered. At its center, business produces new undertakings, setting out positions and open doors for work. These endeavors, going from little and medium-sized undertakings (SMEs) to huge organizations, significantly affect the labor force, animating position creation and diminishing joblessness. Business venture is a powerful driver of nearby work, adding to local area prosperity and feasible development.

The inventive limit of business people is a central part of business' effect on monetary development. Business visionaries are regular issue solvers, continually looking for answers for market holes and failures. Their creative undertakings can prompt the advancement of new items, administrations, and innovations that disturb existing businesses and produce financial worth. Development is a foundation of business venture, driving seriousness and encouraging powerful commercial centers.

Development isn't bound to innovative progressions; it likewise envelops novel plans of action and cycles. Business visionaries frequently challenge conventional techniques for carrying on with work, presenting new methodologies that upgrade effectiveness and decrease costs. These advancements can prompt expanded efficiency and financial development, helping both individual organizations and the more extensive economy.

The formation of new business sectors is an extraordinary result of enterprising development. Business visionaries have the ability to recognize neglected needs and convert them into new items and administrations that take care of already underserved markets.

Thusly, they extend financial open doors and expand businesses. New business sectors extend to pathways for employment opportunity creation and financial turn of events, changing the monetary scene.

As well as creating new pursuits, business venture is an impetus for the improvement of independent companies and new businesses. Independent companies, frequently thought to be the foundation of nearby economies, benefit from the enterprising soul that cultivates development, advancement, and occupation creation. They are dexterous and responsive, strategically set up to tackle pioneering amazing open doors and add to monetary dynamic quality.

The dynamism of business is especially obvious in the domain of innovation and new companies. The innovation area, driven by inventive business people, has disturbed customary enterprises and made completely new business sectors. New companies, with their emphasis on versatility, frequently pioneer pivotal advancements and plans of action, adding to financial development by producing income, making position, and driving development.

The effect of business venture reaches out past monetary development. It assumes a urgent part in friendly turn of events and inclusivity. Business venture can enable underestimated gatherings, offering open doors for financial independence and diminishing disparity. Ladies and minority business people, specifically, have utilized business venture to break obstructions, defeat separation, and accomplish monetary autonomy.

The instructive scene has perceived the extraordinary capability of business. Numerous scholarly establishments offer business programs, empowering and furnishing understudies with the abilities and information to become business visionaries. These projects encourage enterprising reasoning as well as give the important assets and backing to assist hopeful business people with transforming their thoughts into effective endeavors.

While business significantly affects financial development, it likewise faces difficulties that should be addressed to boost its true capacity. Admittance to capital is difficult for some business visionaries. Lying down the vital financing to begin or grow a business can be overwhelming, and the absence of admittance to capital can upset pioneering desires. Drives pointed toward further developing admittance to supporting for business visionaries are basic to filling advancement and financial development.

Administrative weights can likewise present huge difficulties for business vision-aries. Complex allowing processes, unnecessary administration, and cumbersome tax assessment can redirect assets and consideration from useful innovative exercises. Smoothing out guidelines and lessening authoritative obstacles can establish a climate more helpful for business venture.

Business likewise requires risk-taking, and disappointment is an inborn part of innovative undertakings. The anxiety toward disappointment can be an obstruction to possible business people. Supporting daring individuals and giving a security net to the people who adventure into business venture is fundamental to empower develop-ment and financial development.

Development, the cooperative accomplice of business, is a main thrust in molding the cutting edge world. It addresses the turn of events and execution of novel thoughts, cycles, and advances that change enterprises and drive monetary development. The quick speed of mechanical development has reshaped the worldwide monetary scene, upsetting customary plans of action and setting out new open doors.

Development isn't restricted to innovation; it envelops a wide exhibit of areas, from medical services and energy to schooling and assembling. It cultivates innovativeness and critical thinking, prodding progressions that improve efficiency, further develop items and administrations, and open up new business sectors. Developments can be steady, upgrading existing items or cycles, or revolutionary, making altogether new standards and ventures.

The effect of advancement on monetary development is significant. Advancements drive seriousness and monetary worth, empowering organizations to separate them-selves on the lookout. They lead to expanded efficiency, productivity, and produc-tivity, helping individual endeavors and the more extensive economy. Advancements can possibly make totally new ventures, producing position, pay, and monetary development.

Development is likewise a strong impetus for tending to cultural difficulties. Advancements in medical care, for instance, can possibly work on persistent results and decrease medical services costs. Advancements in clean energy and maintainability can drive ecological assurance and monetary development at the same time. Advance-ments in schooling and innovation can democratize admittance to information and abilities, decreasing imbalance and improving labor force availability.

The job of development in making new business sectors is a demonstration of its groundbreaking power. Advancements have the ability to recognize idle market needs and convert them into new items and administrations. These advancements grow financial open doors, enhance enterprises, and make pathways for work creation and monetary turn of events. By recognizing neglected needs and benefiting from pioneer-ing valuable open doors, trend-setters add to monetary energy.

The advanced age has sped up the speed of development, especially in inno-vation and computerized new businesses. The quick advancement of computerized advancements and the web has set out remarkable open doors for business visionaries and pioneers. Innovation new companies have upset conventional ventures, presenting new plans of action, items, and administrations that have reshaped the financial scene.

Development rises above borders and has a worldwide effect. The interconnectedness of the world permits advancements to spread quickly, helping economies around the world. Open development, coordinated effort, and the sharing of information and best practices add to a worldwide culture of advancement, encouraging global collaboration and financial development.

Nonetheless, similar to business venture, development faces difficulties that should be addressed to open its maximum capacity. Protected innovation insurance is a basic worry for trend-setters. Safeguarding protected innovation freedoms is basic to boost development and guarantee trend-setters get fair pay for their endeavors.

Admittance to schooling and preparing is a basic consider cultivating development. Furnishing people with the information, abilities, and assets to enhance is fundamental. Instructive organizations, innovative work subsidizing, and admittance to logical and specialized mastery assume a focal part in supporting development.

Administrative structures can either support or impede advancement. Administrative clearness and adaptability can establish a climate helpful for advancement, while over the top guideline can smother it. Finding some kind of harmony is vital for cultivating advancement while guaranteeing moral and capable turn of events.

Taking everything into account, business and advancement are indivisible drivers of monetary development and progress. Business people recognize potential open doors, assemble assets, and make adventures that create occupations, enhance ventures, and add to nearby and worldwide economies. Advancement, the soul of business, cultivates inventiveness, disturbs conventional ventures, and addresses cultural difficulties.

3.1 Fostering Entrepreneurial Spirit

The enterprising soul is a power of development and monetary dynamism that drives progress and flourishing. It encapsulates the outlook of people who see open doors where others see impediments, who go ahead with well balanced plans of action, and who have the energy and assurance to transform thoughts into the real world. Cultivating the pioneering soul isn't just about making more business visionaries; it's tied in with engaging people and networks to embrace change, make monetary worth, and drive cultural advancement. In this investigation, we dive into the multi-layered parts of cultivating the enterprising soul and what it means for nearby and worldwide economies.

At its center, cultivating the enterprising soul is tied in with developing a climate that urges people to recognize and seek after open doors. It's tied in with imparting a feeling of plausibility, imagination, and self-conviction. Business people are in many cases brought into the world from such conditions, where they figure out how to explore risk, conquer difficulties, and quickly jump all over chances with certainty.

Schooling assumes a crucial part in supporting the enterprising soul. Instructive foundations can act as favorable places for future business people, giving scholastic information as well as the apparatuses and assets important to change thoughts into effective endeavors. Business venture instruction furnishes understudies with the abilities and attitude to distinguish open doors, assess chances, and foster creative arrangements. It cultivates a culture of inventiveness, critical thinking, and versatility.

Business venture instruction can start at different levels, from essential and optional schools to colleges and professional organizations. It ought to envelop a wide range of disciplines, from business and designing to human expression and sociologies. By presenting understudies to different fields and cultivating a multidisciplinary approach, business venture training empowers imagination and the cross-fertilization of thoughts.

Experiential learning is a foundation of business training. Understudies benefit from active encounters, for example, taking part in business rivalries, creating strategies, and taking part in temporary jobs with new companies and private ventures. These pragmatic encounters permit understudies to apply their insight and gain a more profound comprehension of the pioneering system.

Notwithstanding formal schooling, casual learning and mentorship are crucial parts of encouraging the enterprising soul. Effective business people can assume a basic part as coaches, directing hopeful people through the difficulties and vulnerabilities of beginning and growing a business. Mentorship gives significant bits of knowledge, organizations, and true guidance, permitting people to gain from the encounters of the individuals who have strolled the enterprising way.

Admittance to assets and backing is significant for yearning business people. Business hatcheries, gas pedals, and development centers can give a sustaining climate to new companies. They offer admittance to collaborating spaces, subsidizing potential open doors, organizing occasions, and master direction. These assets can fundamentally decrease the obstructions to section for new business visionaries, making it more straightforward for them to seek after their endeavors.

Monetary proficiency is one more essential part of cultivating the innovative soul. Business people should figure out monetary administration, planning, and speculation to pursue informed choices. Monetary instruction can engage people to go with sound monetary decisions and actually deal with the monetary parts of their organizations.

Sustaining the enterprising soul likewise requires a social shift that values risk-taking and versatility. Society ought to celebrate and remunerate advancement, instead of deride disappointment. The apprehension about disappointment can be a critical impediment hoping for business visionaries. A pioneering society that perceives the benefit of gaining from disappointments and views them as venturing stones to progress is fundamental.

Strategy and administrative conditions can altogether affect the pioneering soul. Legislatures can cultivate business by making business-accommodating guidelines, lessening organization, and giving motivators to independent ventures and new companies. Admittance to capital is a basic element, and policymakers ought to zero in on further developing admittance to financing for business people. Moreover, licensed innovation insurance and implementation are fundamental to guarantee that trendsetters can receive the benefits of their manifestations.

Comprehensive and different business venture is a vital part of cultivating the pioneering soul. Business venture ought not be restricted to a specific segment or foundation. Endeavors ought to be made to help and advance business venture among ladies, minorities, and underserved networks. Inclusivity drives monetary development as well as adds to social value.

Globalization and innovation have changed the scene of business venture. The computerized age has democratized admittance to data and assets, empowering business people to begin organizations with insignificant obstructions. Internet business, online commercial centers, and computerized showcasing have opened up new open doors for yearning business people. The worldwide commercial center permits business people to arrive at clients around the world, cultivating global business and exchange.

Social business is one more sign of the enterprising soul. Social business people are driven by a craving to make positive social and natural effect while creating monetary worth. Their endeavors address squeezing cultural issues, like destitution, training, medical services, and natural supportability. Social business venture obscures the lines among benefit and reason, exhibiting the potential for organizations to drive social change.

The idea of enterprise endeavor is acquiring noticeable quality inside bigger associations. Business visionaries are representatives who show pioneering conduct inside their associations, driving development and distinguishing open doors for development. Business undertaking empowers a culture of development and imagination inside companies, permitting them to stay serious and adjust to changing business sector elements.

The job of government and public foundations in encouraging the enterprising soul is urgent. Legislatures ought to put resources into framework, schooling, and advancement to make an environment that upholds business. They can give financing to innovative work, elevate admittance to instruction, and encourage coordinated effort between organizations, scholarly establishments, and exploration focuses.

Public private associations can upgrade the innovative biological system. Joint effort between states, organizations, and common society associations can use assets, information, and organizations to help business venture. These associations can zero in on creating business venture cordial approaches, giving admittance to subsidizing, and advancing advancement.

All in all, encouraging the pioneering soul isn't just about making more business people; about developing an outlook embraces change, jumps all over chances, and makes financial worth. Training, mentorship, admittance to assets, and steady conditions assume fundamental parts in sustaining the enterprising soul. The social shift towards esteeming risk-taking, commending advancement, and gaining from disappointment is critical.

Business venture rises above lines and socioeconomics, driving financial development and social advancement. A power shapes the future and embraces innovation, inclusivity, and social effect. The pioneering soul isn't restricted to new companies and private ventures; it penetrates all parts of society, from training and corporate advancement to worldwide exchange and social change. Encouraging the enterprising soul isn't just an impetus for monetary development yet in addition a way to a more powerful, comprehensive, and creative world. As we explore the intricacies of the 21st 100 years, the pioneering soul will keep on being a directing power in molding what's in store.

3.2 The Role of Innovation in Small-Scale Industries

Limited scope enterprises are many times seen as the essence of neighborhood economies, and development is the backbone that keeps them flourishing and advancing. These endeavors, described by their humble scope and close association with the networks they serve, assume a significant part in producing monetary development, giving work, and encouraging reasonable turn of events. In this investigation, we dive into the fundamental job of advancement in limited scope enterprises, revealing insight into how it enables these organizations, drives seriousness, and energizes monetary advancement.

Limited scope enterprises envelop a great many organizations, from family-claimed stores and neighborhood make studios to specialty producing tasks and imaginative tech new companies. What joins them is their obligation to serving the requirements of their networks and their spryness in adjusting to neighborhood requests. Limited scope businesses, frequently alluded to as Little and Medium-sized Endeavors (SMEs), structure the foundation of numerous nearby economies, contributing in different and significant ways.

Development is a main thrust behind the progress of limited scope enterprises. These organizations are known for their capacity to adjust and answer rapidly to changes in economic situations, purchaser inclinations, and financial patterns. Their ability for development permits them to present new items, administrations, and plans of action that take care of the advancing necessities of their neighborhood markets. Development assists them with remaining cutthroat and important in a high speed worldwide economy.

One of the vital manners by which limited scope enterprises develop is by utilizing their close information on neighborhood networks. They have their fingers on the beat of the neighborhood culture, requirements, and inclinations, permitting them to foster remarkable items and administrations that reverberate with the local area.

This limited way to deal with development prompts the production of merchandise and arrangements that are more custom-made to the nearby culture and climate, eventually giving an upper hand.

Neighborhood organizations frequently fill market holes and address neglected needs through development. They have the adaptability to perceive arising patterns and changes in purchaser conduct, permitting them to foster items and administrations that take care of these progressions quickly. This responsiveness to nearby requests positions limited scope ventures as innovators, impacting the neighborhood market scene and driving customer decisions.

Development in limited scope enterprises goes past making items; it stretches out to the manner in which they carry on with work. A significant number of these undertakings take on imaginative plans of action, creation cycles, and showcasing systems that streamline their tasks. They smooth out their cycles to diminish costs and further develop productivity, frequently with an eye toward maintainability and asset protection.

Supportability is a central element of development in limited scope enterprises. Their nearby association with neighborhood networks frequently prompts a personal stake in safeguarding the climate and guaranteeing the prosperity of the area. Independent companies oftentimes embrace manageable practices, like decreasing waste, preserving assets, and supporting nearby drives for ecological insurance. This obligation to manageability lines up with the developing accentuation on green and moral strategic policies, making limited scope enterprises fundamental supporters of dependable financial development.

In many examples, limited scope businesses assume a significant part in local area improvement through their imaginative methodologies. They give potential open doors to neighborhood business and business venture, encouraging a healthy identity adequacy and adding to local area prosperity. This obligation to neighborhood advancement frequently reaches out to socially dependable drives, like supporting schooling, medical care, and social conservation in their networks.

Neighborhood private companies are profoundly implanted in the texture of their networks, frequently assuming a focal part in saving social customs and nearby personality. They produce labor and products that mirror the novel attributes and legacy of their networks, adding to the protection of social customs and practices. By supporting nearby craftsmanship and social exercises, limited scope enterprises become watchmen of a locale's character and history.

Moreover, the flexibility of limited scope businesses frequently depends on their capacity to enhance. They are better prepared to endure financial slumps and interruptions due to their flexibility. This flexibility is especially clear in the midst of emergencies, like the new Coronavirus pandemic. Independent companies, including nearby eateries, create makers, and specialty retailers, showed their strength by rapidly turning their tasks to address the issues of the local area during the pandemic.

In any case, advancement in limited scope enterprises isn't without its difficulties. Admittance to capital is a huge obstacle for some business visionaries. Restricted monetary assets can impede the development and extension of these organizations. Numerous entrepreneurs battle to get credits or speculations, which can smother development and extension. The absence of admittance to capital additionally restricts their capacity to put resources into innovative work, hampering their seriousness and capacity to quickly jump all over development chances.

Deficient framework, including restricted admittance to solid power, transportation, and correspondence organizations, can likewise represent a critical obstruction for limited scope ventures. These inadequacies can increment creation costs and confine market reach, making it more hard for these undertakings to contend for a bigger scope. Admittance to present day foundation is in many cases a basic consider deciding the seriousness and development capability of limited scope businesses.

Administrative obstacles address one more huge test for limited scope enterprises. Extreme organization, complex allowing processes, and burdensome tax assessment can be overpowering for entrepreneurs, redirecting assets from useful exercises and into managerial obstacles. At times, these guidelines can prompt casualness, as business visionaries decide to work under the table to stay away from the intricacies and expenses of consistence. Administrative change and improvement are pivotal for upgrading the development possibilities of limited scope enterprises.

The worldwide commercial center, portrayed by wild rivalry and innovative progressions, presents a significant test to limited scope businesses. In a climate where economies of scale frequently decide achievement, these organizations might battle to stay up with bigger enterprises. The absence of assets for innovative work can frustrate their capacity to embrace current advancements, robotize processes, and contend successfully.

Notwithstanding these difficulties, the inventive soul of limited scope ventures continues. Their capacity to adjust, serve neighborhood networks, and cultivate manageable practices makes them significant supporters of nearby and public economies. They are centers of inventiveness, social safeguarding, and social prosperity, forming the character and flourishing of their networks.

3.3 Profiles of Innovative Entrepreneurs

Development is the foundation of enterprising achievement, driving change, making financial worth, and molding ventures. The accounts of creative business visionaries from different foundations give important experiences into the qualities, attitude, and approaches that fuel their prosperity. In this investigation, we dig into the profiles of a few creative business visionaries who have made an enduring imprint on their particular enterprises, revealing the elements that put them aside and the illustrations they proposition desiring business visionaries.

Elon Musk: The Visionary of Room Investigation

Elon Musk is a visionary business person known for his noteworthy work in the fields of aviation, electric vehicles, and sustainable power. He helped to establish Zip2, a web-based professional listing, which he sold for $307 million out of 1999. This early achievement gave the monetary establishment to his resulting adventures, which would groundbreakingly affect the world.

Musk established SpaceX in 2002 determined to diminish the expense of room investigation and making Mars colonization a reality. SpaceX has accomplished various achievements, including sending off the first secretly subsidized rocket into space and giving reasonable space transportation. Musk's persevering quest for development and his eagerness to face challenges have situated SpaceX as an innovator in the aeronautic trade.

One more of Musk's outstanding endeavors is Tesla, an organization devoted to creating electric vehicles and practical energy arrangements. Under his administration, Tesla changed the car business by advocating electric vehicles and accomplishing huge headways in battery innovation. Musk's emphasis on manageability and his readiness to challenge conventional auto producers have made Tesla a commonly recognized name.

Musk's vocation is set apart by his capacity to imagine aggressive objectives, proceed with reasonable plans of action, and drive advancement in numerous enterprises at the same time. His endeavors have reclassified conceivable outcomes in space investigation, electric vehicles, and environmentally friendly power, exhibiting the force of a visionary business person with a steady quest for development.

Oprah Winfrey: The News Investor and Humanitarian

Oprah Winfrey is a notorious figure in the media and media outlet, celebrated for her powerful syndicated program, "The Oprah Winfrey Show." She conquered a provoking childhood to turn into a news tycoon, humanitarian, and supporter for social causes.

Winfrey's inventive way to deal with TV syndicated programs put her aside. She carried profundity and genuineness to her meetings, handling a large number of themes, from self improvement and self-awareness to social issues and governmental issues. Her capacity to interface with her crowd on an individual level and address pertinent issues made her show a stage for change and strengthening.

Notwithstanding her TV profession, Winfrey has wandered into different organizations, including sending off her telecom company, OWN (Oprah Winfrey Organization). Her impact reaches out past media, as she has effectively taken part in charity and support. She established the Oprah Winfrey Authority Foundation for Young ladies in South Africa, giving instructive open doors to oppressed young ladies.

Winfrey's creative way to deal with narrating and her capacity to resolve significant issues through media have procured her an exceptional situation in media outlets

She has exhibited the force of validness and sympathy in associating with crowds and driving positive change.

Steve Occupations: The Mac Visionary

Steve Occupations, the fellow benefactor of Mac Inc., was an imaginative business visionary known for his unprecedented commitments to the innovation and purchaser gadgets ventures. His imaginative vision and firm quest for greatness did great things.

Macintosh, under Positions' initiative, presented historic items that changed ventures. The Mac PC, iPod, iPhone, and iPad are only a couple of instances of his developments. Occupations was prestigious for his thoughtfulness regarding plan, usefulness, and client experience. He altered how individuals communicated with innovation, making it more natural and available.

Occupations' obligation to development reached out past items to plans of action. He embraced the idea of the "Apple biological system," making a consistent combination of equipment, programming, and administrations. This biological system improved client experience as well as drove client dependability and income development.

Occupations' readiness to face challenges and rock the boat was a main impetus behind his prosperity. His enterprising excursion was set apart by various difficulties and misfortunes, yet he never faltered in his obligation to advancement. His persevering quest for flawlessness and his capacity to imagine items that shoppers didn't realize they needed put him aside as an innovative symbol.

Arianna Huffington: The Media Expert and Wellbeing Backer

Arianna Huffington is a prestigious media business person, creator, and backer for prosperity. She helped to establish The Huffington Post, a notable news and assessment site, which she later offered to AOL for $315 million. Her inventive way to deal with online media and her obligation to advancing prosperity have been integral to her innovative excursion.

The Huffington Post upset the conventional media scene by giving a stage to different voices and suppositions. Its imaginative model of joining proficient reporting with commitments from a great many essayists democratized the media scene. This approach tested the idea that customary news sources were the sole judges of information and data.

Huffington's obligation to prosperity and the significance of rest prompted the formation of Flourish Worldwide, an organization committed to advancing wellbeing and health. Flourish Worldwide's central goal is to end the burnout culture by giving people and associations instruments and techniques for prosperity. Huffington's pioneering venture is described by her imaginative way to deal with media and her devotion to working on individuals' lives.

Jeff Bezos: The Online business Trailblazer

Jeff Bezos is the organizer behind Amazon, an organization that has re-imagined internet business, distributed computing, and computerized content dissemination. His inventive vision and determined client center have made Amazon one of the world's most powerful and fruitful innovation organizations.

Bezos established Amazon in 1994 as a web-based book shop, however he immediately extended its item contributions and changed it into an online business goliath. His client driven approach, exemplified by drives like Amazon Prime and a single tick requesting, made internet shopping more helpful and open to a worldwide crowd.

Bezos' inventive outlook stretched out to Amazon Web Administrations (AWS), the organization's distributed computing division. AWS has turned into a main supplier of cloud foundation and administrations, serving organizations and associations around the world. Bezos' obligation to driving advancement and proficiency in distributed computing has reshaped the innovation scene.

Bezos' enterprising excursion is set apart by his capacity to expect customer needs and convey inventive arrangements. His tireless quest for comfort, cost-productivity, and consumer loyalty has situated Amazon as a worldwide forerunner in web based business and innovation.

Illustrations from Creative Business visionaries

These profiles of imaginative business people offer important examples and experiences for hopeful business pioneers:

Vision and Tirelessness: Creative business people share areas of strength for an and an unfaltering obligation to their objectives. They are not stopped by difficulties and misfortunes, and they persevere even with affliction.

Client Driven Approach: Consumer loyalty and understanding are integral to their plans of action. They endeavor to address buyer issues and convey items and administrations that work on individuals' lives.

Different Ways to deal with Development: Advancement takes different structures, from reconsidering client encounters to making troublesome items or administrations. Business visionaries can develop in both item and plan of action perspectives.

Social Effect: Numerous creative business people utilize their prosperity as a stage to advocate for social causes, advance prosperity, and have a beneficial outcome on society.

Risk-Taking: Business frequently implies carefully weighed out courses of action. Effective business visionaries will face challenges to accomplish their objectives, even notwithstanding vulnerability.

Variety and Inclusivity: Embracing different viewpoints and democratizing admittance to assets can prompt creative arrangements and plans of action that take special care of a more extensive crowd.

Chapter 4

Economic Diversity through Small Businesses

Private companies are the foundation of any economy, assuming an essential part in encouraging monetary variety, development, and occupation creation. In the cutting edge world, as enormous partnerships rule titles and worldwide business sectors, neglecting the meaning of private companies is simple. However, these ventures are the backbone of numerous nearby and public economies, filling in as a strong power for financial variety.

One of the most essential parts of independent ventures is their capacity to give financial variety inside a local area or country. They frequently address a great many ventures, from retail and neighborliness to innovation new businesses and specialist organizations. By offering different labor and products, independent ventures add to the generally speaking financial flexibility, diminishing the gamble of overreliance on a solitary industry or area. This enhancement is crucial, as it helps pad the economy against outer shocks and interruptions.

Besides, private companies are many times more versatile and receptive to showcase changes contrasted with their bigger partners. They can rapidly change their techniques, items, and administrations in light of moving shopper inclinations or monetary circumstances. This deftness is a vital driver of financial variety, as it empowers development and rivalry, eventually prompting better items and administrations.

Private ventures likewise encourage financial variety by giving open positions across a wide range of abilities and foundations. Not at all like enormous organizations, which frequently look for profoundly particular skill, independent ventures recruit from a more different ability pool. They set out work open doors for people with differing levels of involvement and schooling, which adds to a more comprehensive and impartial labor force.

Besides, private ventures are in many cases profoundly implanted in their networks. They are bound to source materials and administrations locally, which helps support other private companies, making a multiplier impact. This interconnected snare of independent ventures fortifies the neighborhood economy, prompting monetary variety through common help and reliance.

The significance of private ventures in advancing monetary variety is obvious in their huge commitment to work. In the US, for instance, private ventures represented 44% of absolute financial action in 2021 and produced 65% of net new positions somewhere in the range of 2000 and 2021. These measurements highlight the imperative job of private ventures in making a different and strong work market.

Private companies likewise drive advancement, one more essential component of monetary variety. Their more modest size frequently considers more trial and error and hazard taking. They can put up groundbreaking thoughts and items for sale to the public quicker than bigger companies, which are frequently troubled by administration and hazard avoidance. This development effectively enhances the monetary scene by presenting new areas and advances.

Moreover, independent ventures frequently cultivate a culture of business and imagination. By moving people to begin their own undertakings, they add to a powerful climate where new thoughts and business ideas can flourish. The combined impact of these new companies is a more extravagant and more different monetary environment.

Nonetheless, private ventures face various provokes in their mission to advance financial variety. Admittance to capital is a critical obstacle. Numerous business visionaries battle to tie down financing to begin or extend their organizations, which restricts their development potential and ability to differentiate the economy. This issue is intensified by the way that bigger monetary organizations might be more disposed to loan to laid out enterprises, leaving independent ventures in a difficult spot.

Administrative and regulatory weights can likewise be a boundary to monetary variety through private companies. Exploring complex guidelines and guidelines can be especially trying for new business people, making it harder for them to contend and improve. Smoothing out and improving on these cycles can assist with evening the odds and support greater variety in the business scene.

Furthermore, admittance to reasonable medical care and different advantages is a worry for the majority entrepreneurs and their workers. These variables can obstruct the development of private companies and keep people from seeking after business venture, decreasing the potential for financial variety.

One more test looked by private ventures is the lopsided effect of financial slumps. During seasons of emergency, private companies are many times more defenseless than enormous organizations, prompting terminations and employment misfortunes. This weakness can disturb the financial variety that independent ventures add to, accentuating the requirement for designated help and arrangements to reinforce their flexibility.

In numerous nations, government drives and projects exist to help private ventures and advance financial variety. These endeavors incorporate monetary help, admittance to preparing and assets, and duty impetuses. Legislatures perceive the significance of private ventures in making a more different and vigorous economy and expect to give the vital devices to them to flourish.

Cooperative endeavors between private ventures and instructive foundations can likewise add to financial variety. By encouraging organizations with colleges and professional schools, private ventures can assist with forming educational plans and furnish understudies with true encounters, guaranteeing that graduates are more ready to add to the different monetary scene.

Private ventures have shown to be especially versatile during the Coronavirus pandemic. Many adjusted rapidly to new circumstances by turning their plans of action, offering on the web administrations, and tracking down innovative ways of keeping on serving their networks. This versatility highlights their importance in keeping up with financial variety even in the midst of emergency.

Advancing monetary variety through private ventures isn't restricted to any single industry or area. Whether it's a local bread shop, a tech startup, or a nearby specialist co-op, every independent venture adds to a more fluctuated and strong economy. Their job is particularly vital in encouraging inclusivity and equivalent open doors for people from various foundations.

All in all, private ventures assume a significant part in advancing financial variety by offering a different scope of labor and products, making position across different expertise levels, and encouraging development. Notwithstanding the difficulties they face, independent companies are a basic power for differentiating the economy and upgrading its flexibility. It is basic for legislatures, instructive organizations, and the more extensive local area to keep supporting private ventures and perceiving their significance in molding a more unique and comprehensive financial scene. The proceeded with progress of independent ventures is fundamental for the general wellbeing and dynamic quality of our economies and social orders.

4.1 Diverse Sectors and Industries

The worldwide economy is a complicated and interconnected framework including a huge range of areas and businesses. The variety of these areas is a central strength, guaranteeing security, versatility, and development inside economies. Various areas incorporate an expansive range of exercises, from assembling and horticulture to innovation, medical care, money, and that's just the beginning. This variety is basic for monetary development and improvement, as it makes a fair biological system that can adjust to different difficulties and changes.

One of the essential advantages of having assorted areas and ventures is the versatility it offers to the general economy. At the point when one area encounters a slump or interruption, different areas can go about as a cushion, assisting with balancing out the economy.

For example, during a downturn, while the assembling area may be battling, the medical care or administration businesses could in any case be flourishing. This broadening limits the gamble of a complete monetary breakdown and adds to a more steady climate for organizations and people.

Besides, various areas and ventures invigorate development. Every area has its remarkable arrangement of difficulties, which frequently prompts the advancement of new innovations, cycles, and arrangements. For example, mechanical headways in the medical care area, for example, telemedicine and creative clinical gadgets, further develop medical care conveyance as well as have applications in different ventures. This cross-fertilization of thoughts across areas cultivates a culture of development that impels financial development.

The work open doors given by different areas are significant. Various businesses take care of fluctuated ranges of abilities, instructive foundations, and interests. This inclusivity in open positions helps in decreasing joblessness rates and guarantees a more different and gifted labor force. Areas like farming, assembling, innovation, and administrations all require unmistakable gifts, adding to a balanced and versatile labor force.

One more huge benefit of assorted areas and businesses is the formation of reliance. Areas frequently depend on one another for provisions, administrations, or mastery. For example, the rural area supplies unrefined substances to the food handling industry, which, thusly, gives items to the retail and accommodation areas. This reliance fortifies the economy as well as supports joint effort and collaboration among areas, encouraging a more strong business climate.

In any case, while the variety of areas brings various benefits, it likewise presents difficulties. Monetary association between areas can prompt weaknesses. An emergency in one area can have a flowing impact, affecting others in the store network. The Coronavirus pandemic clearly exhibited this interconnectivity, where the closure of enterprises like travel and friendliness fundamentally impacted different areas, from assembling to transportation.

Another test originates from the fast development of innovation and mechanization. While mechanical progressions have prompted expanded efficiency and productivity, they have likewise caused disturbances in different areas, prompting position uprooting and the requirement for upskilling or retraining the labor force. The steady requirement for transformation and development in light of mechanical changes is a ceaseless test across areas.

Worldwide monetary abberations and lopsided improvement across areas and ventures present another test. In numerous economies, certain areas prosper while others fall behind because of different factors like government arrangements, foundation, or market interest. This lopsided development can make irregular characteristics and prevent the generally speaking monetary strength and variety.

Tending to these difficulties requires a thorough methodology that includes co-operation between legislatures, organizations, and different partners. Legislatures can assume a vital part in cultivating variety across areas by executing strategies that empower development and offer help for enterprises confronting difficulties. They can likewise put resources into foundation and schooling to help the development of different areas, guaranteeing a decent and various economy.

Organizations likewise have an obligation to adjust and improve inside their areas. Embracing mechanical progressions, advancing feasible practices, and putting resources into the labor force's ability improvement are fundamental stages toward guaranteeing the versatility and development of different areas. Joint effort and organizations between organizations inside and across areas can likewise drive advancement and development.

Schooling and labor force improvement programs are basic in getting ready people for different areas and enterprises. Giving admittance to quality instruction and professional preparation custom-made to the necessities of different areas outfits people with the vital abilities and information to contribute successfully to a different economy. Long lasting learning and flexibility become key in guaranteeing the labor force stays cutthroat and important across evolving areas.

The advancement of manageability is progressively becoming interlaced with assorted areas and enterprises. The emphasis on harmless to the ecosystem rehearses and environmentally friendly power sources is reshaping businesses, affecting areas to adjust to additional reasonable models. This shift helps the climate as well as sets out new open doors and enterprises, subsequently adding to a more different financial scene.

The consistently developing computerized economy is likewise reshaping assorted areas and enterprises. The coordination of innovation is turning into a principal perspective across areas, prompting the ascent of new ventures like internet business, computerized promoting, and network protection. This reconciliation cultivates further variety and guarantees flexibility in an undeniably interconnected world.

All in all, the variety of areas and businesses is a foundation of a hearty and versatile economy. It brings dependability, cultivates development, sets out business open doors, and supports reliance among various areas. Challenges like financial relationship, mechanical interruptions, and worldwide differences should be tended to cooperatively by states, organizations, and instructive foundations. Embracing mechanical progressions, advancing maintainability, and putting resources into training and labor force advancement are fundamental procedures in guaranteeing the ceaseless development and versatility of assorted areas and ventures. A dynamic, comprehensive, and various financial scene is critical for supported development and flourishing in a consistently developing worldwide economy.

4.2 Benefits of Economic Diversity

Monetary variety, portrayed by the presence of many areas and ventures inside an economy, offers a huge number of benefits that add to soundness, strength, and in general thriving. A different economy isn't dependent on a solitary industry, making it less defenseless against monetary shocks and disturbances. It empowers development, gives work open doors across different ranges of abilities, and cultivates association among areas. In this conversation, we will investigate the various advantages of financial variety and its positive effect on people, organizations, and society at large.

1. **Strength and Security**

   One of the essential advantages of monetary variety is the versatility it bestows to an economy. At the point when an economy depends vigorously on a solitary industry, it turns out to be exceptionally helpless against outer shocks or slumps well defined for that area. Interestingly, a different economy has numerous areas that can go about as a cradle against monetary emergencies. On the off chance that one area encounters a slump, others might stay steady or even flourish. This enhancement mitigates the gamble of a horrendous financial breakdown, giving a wellbeing net to organizations and people.

   For instance, during the 2008 monetary emergency, economies with different areas were better prepared to face the hardship. While the monetary area confronted huge difficulties, different ventures, like medical services, innovation, and assembling, proceeded to develop and give business open doors, hence forestalling a total financial implosion.

2. **Advancement and Cross-Fertilization of Thoughts**

   Monetary variety invigorates development by encouraging a culture of inventiveness and critical thinking across different areas. Every industry faces novel difficulties and requests, which frequently lead to the advancement of new innovations, cycles, and arrangements. These developments are not bound to their separate areas; they frequently have applications in different enterprises, advancing cross-fertilization of thoughts and mechanical headways.

   For instance, progressions in advanced mechanics produced for assembling have tracked down applications in medical care, horticulture, and operations. This sort of advancement could never have been conceivable without the assorted arrangement of difficulties presented by various areas.

3. **Business Amazing open doors**

   Various areas and enterprises give an extensive variety of work valuable open doors. Various businesses require different ranges of abilities, instructive foundations, and mastery, making it workable for people to secure positions that line up with their capabilities and interests. This inclusivity in open positions lessens joblessness rates as well as guarantees a more different and talented labor force. Whether it's assembling, horticulture, innovation, medical care, or administrations, every area adds to the formation of a balanced and versatile labor force. This variety permits people to seek after professions that match their abilities and interests, prompting more noteworthy work fulfillment and efficiency.

4. **Association and Coordinated effort**

   Monetary variety encourages reliance among areas, as they frequently depend on one another for provisions, administrations, or mastery. This interconnectedness reinforces the economy and supports joint effort and participation among areas. At the point when one area thrives, it emphatically influences others in the store network, prompting common development and success.

For example, the farming area supplies natural substances to the food handling industry, which, thus, gives items to the retail and friendliness areas. This relationship not just guarantees a steady progression of labor and products yet additionally upholds the development of related organizations.

5. **Moderation of Chance and Vulnerability**

Various areas assist with moderating gamble and vulnerability by decreasing an economy's reliance on a solitary industry or market. At the point when a nation depends vigorously on one area for its financial prosperity, it turns out to be profoundly vulnerable to vacillations in that area, like changes in worldwide interest or market unpredictability. Monetary variety scatters risk, making it doubtful that the whole economy will experience the ill effects of area explicit difficulties.

For instance, consider a country that intensely relies upon oil creation. Assuming that oil costs dive because of worldwide occasions, the whole economy would be in peril. Conversely, a broadened economy would have different areas adding to its Gross domestic product, making it stronger despite falling oil costs.

6. **Venture Open doors**

Monetary variety draws in a more extensive scope of financial backers and monetary open doors. Financial backers will generally incline toward economies that display versatility and dependability, as they offer a more secure climate for their ventures. Various economies will generally be more alluring to unfamiliar direct venture (FDI) as they offer a more steady and secure speculation climate.

Also, financial variety frequently prompts the production of new organizations and areas. These arising ventures can be rich ground for business visionaries and financial backers searching for learning experiences. This draws in homegrown speculations as well as urges unfamiliar cash-flow to stream into the economy, further reinforcing financial turn of events.

7. **Monetary Fairness and Inclusivity**

Different areas and enterprises add to financial balance and inclusivity by giving open positions to people from different foundations, expertise levels, and instructive fulfillments. The assorted labor force that rises up out of various areas helps span financial holes, guaranteeing that individuals from different foundations approach work and monetary open doors.

For instance, an assorted economy can offer situations for people with various degrees of schooling and experience. An assembling organization could give occupations to talented merchants, while the innovation area could enlist computer programmers. This inclusivity advances monetary fairness and permits people to seek after vocation ways that line up with their abilities and desires.

8. **Ecological Maintainability**

Progressively, monetary variety is related with manageability. As the world wrestles with ecological difficulties, various areas and enterprises take into consideration the coordination of maintainable practices and the advancement of harmless to the ecosystem innovations. These practices benefit the climate as well as set out new open doors and ventures, further adding to monetary variety. Areas like environmentally friendly power, green innovation, and supportable farming are arising as fundamental parts of different economies. By focusing on manageability, different economies advance natural obligation and decrease the ecological effect of modern exercises.

9. **Versatility to Innovative Change**

In the present quickly developing mechanical scene, different areas are better situated to adjust to innovative changes and disturbances. The joining of innovation into different ventures is a sign of an assorted economy, guaranteeing that organizations stay cutthroat and important in an undeniably interconnected world.

Ventures like internet business, advanced advertising, and network safety have arisen as huge parts of different economies. The capacity to embrace mechanical progressions and adjust to changing purchaser inclinations is a critical benefit of having different areas.

10. **Social and Social Variety**

Monetary variety frequently prompts social and social variety inside a district or country. As different businesses draw in people with various foundations and skill, a multicultural and different society arises. This social wealth can prompt a more lively and dynamic culture, encouraging social trade and inventiveness.

For instance, a locale with a flourishing innovation area might draw in ability from around the world, making a different and cosmopolitan local area. This variety improves the social texture as well as advances social trade and resistance.

11. **Rustic Metropolitan Equilibrium**

Financial variety can assist with finding some kind of harmony among metropolitan and provincial regions. It gives business open doors in both metropolitan and provincial settings, lessening the convergence of financial action in significant urban communities. This geographic variety adds to the improvement of framework, administrations, and conveniences in different locales, eventually helping a more extensive range of the populace.

Different areas and businesses frequently incorporate agribusiness, which gives jobs in country regions, as well as innovation and administrations that are pervasive in metropolitan habitats. This equilibrium can assist with balancing the difficulties of country eradication and metropolitan congestion.

12. **Long haul Monetary Development**

    Financial variety is helpful for maintained, long haul monetary development. A different economy is better prepared to adjust to evolving conditions, quickly jump all over new chances, and enhance, in this manner guaranteeing proceeded with financial extension. This development emphatically influences expectations for everyday comforts, framework improvement, and generally speaking flourishing.

    Different economies are bound to encounter consistent development over the long run, as they are not under obligation to the exhibition of a solitary area or industry. This financial strength establishes a good climate for organizations and people to contribute, plan for the future, and add to the by and large monetary prosperity of the country.

13. **Encouraging Business venture**

    Different areas and enterprises encourage business venture by establishing a powerful climate where groundbreaking thoughts and business ideas can flourish. As various areas connect and impact one another, business people are given chances to distinguish holes, improve, and begin new organizations. This pioneering society is fundamental for financial variety and energizes the making of new companies and private ventures that add to work creation and development.

    ### 4.3 Encouraging Niche Businesses

    Specialty organizations, described by their specialization in serving an unmistakable market or tending to a specific need, assume an imperative part in the present economy. While they may not have the scale or perceivability of bigger, more summed up endeavors, these organizations offer novel benefits that add to monetary variety, development, and the general prosperity of networks. In this conversation, we will investigate the significance of empowering specialty organizations, their effect on neighborhood and worldwide economies, and techniques to help their development and achievement.

1. **Cultivating Monetary Variety**

   Specialty organizations are fundamental parts of monetary variety. They change up an economy by zeroing in on particular items or administrations. These organizations take care of explicit client portions, necessities, or inclinations, which may not be satisfactorily tended to by bigger, more broad contenders. Subsequently, they add to a broadened financial scene that is stronger and versatile to change.

   Specialty organizations frequently flourish in regions that fall outside the standard. By offering novel items or administrations, they give choices to efficiently manufactured, one-size-fits-all contributions. This variety can be a life saver during monetary slumps or emergencies, as specialty organizations will more often than not hold a faithful client base in any event, when bigger partnerships experience declines.

2. **Empowering Development**

Specialty organizations are regular favorable places for development. Their specialization requires a profound comprehension of their particular market or industry, and this skill frequently prompts imaginative critical thinking and exceptional arrangements. More modest, more particular groups can turn rapidly in light of market requests or arising patterns, cultivating a culture of persistent improvement and development.

Additionally, specialty organizations frequently track down motivation and thoughts by recognizing neglected needs or holes on the lookout. By offering specific items or administrations that take care of these neglected necessities, they can disturb laid out enterprises and open up new open doors for advancement and business.

3. **Improving Neighborhood Economies**

Specialty organizations can fundamentally affect neighborhood economies. They frequently source their materials or work locally, subsequently supporting different organizations and making a multiplier impact. As they develop, they add to the improvement of a nearby environment that cultivates monetary variety and strength.

Moreover, specialty organizations can go about as magnets, attracting clients and vacationers who look for exceptional and particular encounters. Nearby economies can profit from expanded pedestrian activity and the travel industry, prompting extra deals for reciprocal organizations like cafés, inns, and transportation administrations.

4. **Advancing Business venture**

Empowering specialty organizations advances business venture. Numerous people are attracted to beginning their own particular endeavor that lines up with their interests and mastery. These specialty business people drive development and add to the financial texture by carrying new thoughts and ways to deal with their particular fields.

Supporting specialty business venture can prompt a rush of new organizations, setting out work open doors, invigorating nearby economies, and adding to a different and dynamic business scene.

5. **Meeting Assorted Client Needs**

Specialty organizations succeed in tending to explicit client needs. While bigger companies frequently go for the gold allure, specialty organizations can offer custom-made, top notch items or administrations that take care of a specialty crowd with unmistakable inclinations or necessities.

For instance, a little distinctive bread shop could have some expertise in sans gluten cakes, taking care of people with dietary limitations. This specialty bread shop can offer better quality and consideration than detail, settling on it the go-to decision for those with gluten awarenesses. By zeroing in on such concentrated specialties, organizations can fabricate a dedicated client base and make a specialty explicit brand character.

6. **Manageability and Neighborhood Creation**

Numerous specialty organizations focus on supportable and neighborhood creation rehearses. They might utilize privately obtained materials, diminish squander, and underscore harmless to the ecosystem processes. By lining up with these qualities, specialty organizations add to supportability and advance eco-cognizant utilization.

Besides, by underscoring neighborhood creation and obtaining, specialty organizations can lessen the carbon impression related with transportation and strategies. This approach isn't just earth dependable yet in addition reverberates with shoppers who focus on maintainable practices.

7. **Contest and Market Elements**

Specialty organizations bring solid contest into the market. They can disturb laid out businesses by offering specific other options, giving decisions to buyers, and empowering bigger enterprises to adjust and enhance to fulfill the changing business sector needs. Solid rivalry adds to customer strengthening and upgraded item quality.

For example, the rise of specialty electric vehicle makers has driven laid out car monsters to put all the more vigorously in electric and maintainable innovation. This opposition has sped up the change toward all the more harmless to the ecosystem transportation choices.

8. **Customized Client Experience**

Specialty organizations frequently offer a customized client experience that goes past what bigger, more summed up organizations can give. They have the adaptability to tailor their contributions, adjust to client inclinations, and assemble cozy associations with their client base. This customized touch makes a feeling of local area and dependability among clients.

Little, specialty organizations regularly draw in with their clients on an individual level, whether through direct correspondence, customization of items or administrations, or facilitating local area occasions. This approach encourages client trust and improves the general client experience.

9. **Work Creation and Business Open doors**

Specialty organizations assume a pivotal part in work creation, both straightforwardly and in a roundabout way. These organizations frequently start little, utilizing a center group of specialists who drive their specialization. As they extend and succeed, they require extra staff, adding to business open doors inside their networks.

Moreover, specialty organizations make a far reaching influence in work creation through their effect on the nearby economy. As they develop, they support providers, specialist co-ops, and other reciprocal organizations, further upgrading work open doors in different areas.

10. **Local area Personality and Realness**

Specialty organizations add to the extraordinary character and credibility of networks. They frequently mirror the way of life, legacy, and upsides of their neighborhood locales, adding character and flavor to the local area. This social legitimacy can be a huge draw for travelers and guests, adding to the neighborhood economy.

For instance, a little winery in a country region could have some expertise in creating wines special to the nearby terroir, commending the locale's unmistakable flavors and customs. Vacationers are attracted to such specialty organizations, looking for a real encounter that interfaces them to the nearby culture.

11. **Custom-made Answers for Complex Difficulties**

Now and again, specialty organizations give specific answers for complex difficulties. They frequently arise as a reaction to interesting or neglected needs inside a specific market or industry. Their inside and out comprehension of these difficulties permits them to foster exact, powerful arrangements.

For instance, in the field of medical care, particular telemedicine organizations take special care of patients with uncommon ailments who might require the mastery of a particular trained professional. These specialty organizations associate patients with the right medical services experts, offering customized arrangements that may not be promptly accessible through customary medical care suppliers.

12. **Adjusting to Changing Customer Inclinations**

Customer inclinations are persistently advancing, and specialty organizations are much of the time more deft in adjusting to these changes. Their more modest size and specialization empower them to turn rapidly and answer arising patterns, client requests, and cultural movements.

For instance, a little beauty care products organization spend significant time in clean excellence items can quickly change its plans to satisfy developing shopper needs for normal and feasible fixings. This flexibility positions specialty organizations as innovators that take care of developing inclinations.

13. **Nearby Distinctive and Art Customs**

Specialty organizations frequently center around protecting and advancing neighborhood distinctive and make customs. They make a business opportunity for hand tailored, extraordinary, and excellent items that might be in danger of vanishing despite large scale manufacturing and globalization.

For example, a little earthenware studio could deliver handmade ceramics utilizing customary strategies went down through ages. Thusly, they support nearby craftsmans and assist with supporting social practices while offering clients one of a kind and legitimate items.

| 46 |

Chapter 5

Challenges Faced by Small-Scale Industries

Limited scope enterprises assume a pivotal part in the financial improvement of a country. They are much of the time seen as the foundation of an economy, contributing altogether to business age, monetary development, and industrialization. In any case, these endeavors are not without their reasonable part of difficulties. In this conversation, we will dig into the diverse difficulties looked by limited scope ventures and their suggestions on these organizations and the more extensive economy.

One of the essential difficulties experienced by limited scope businesses is restricted admittance to back. These organizations frequently battle to tie down the fundamental cash-flow to start or extend their tasks. Monetary organizations, especially conventional banks, are frequently hesitant to loan to limited scope endeavors because of seen gambles and insufficient guarantee. This absence of admittance to capital can smother development and cutoff the capability of these organizations. Some limited scale business visionaries resort to costly casual wellsprings of money, for example, moneylenders, which can prompt a pattern of obligation and monetary unsteadiness.

Notwithstanding monetary imperatives, limited scope enterprises face a huge number of administrative and consistence challenges. States frequently force a complicated trap of guidelines and permitting prerequisites, making it challenging for these endeavors to explore the regulatory labyrinth. Consistence with work regulations, ecological guidelines, and duty commitments can be especially troublesome. Limited scope business visionaries might come up short on assets and mastery to deal with these necessities successfully, prompting lawful issues and functional interruptions. Working on administrative techniques and offering help in consistence can fundamentally lighten this test.

Another huge test is the absence of current innovation and framework. Limited scope enterprises frequently work with obsolete apparatus and innovation, which hampers their efficiency and intensity. Restricted admittance to solid foundation, like transportation and utilities, can additionally obstruct their activities. Redesigning innovation and framework can be costly, and limited scope organizations might battle to make the fundamental ventures. States and industry affiliations can assume a fundamental part in giving admittance to present day innovation and further developing framework for these endeavors.

Market access and rivalry present one more arrangement of difficulties. Limited scope enterprises face serious contest, both from other limited scope organizations and bigger companies. They frequently come up short on assets to showcase their items really or extend their client base. Admittance to homegrown and worldwide business sectors can be confined because of exchange hindrances, absence of market data, and deficient dissemination organizations. Creating promoting and dispersion systems, also as exchange help measures, can assist limited scope enterprises with defeating these difficulties and access bigger business sectors.

Human asset the executives is likewise difficult for limited scope ventures. Finding and holding gifted work can be troublesome, as bigger organizations frequently extend to more alluring remuneration bundles and employment opportunity security. Limited scope endeavors might battle to give preparing and improvement open doors to their representatives, prompting expertise holes and diminished efficiency. Empowering expertise improvement, offering cutthroat wages, and establishing a favorable workplace can assist with tending to these human asset challenges.

Admittance to natural substances and inventory network issues can altogether influence limited scope businesses. These organizations might confront challenges in obtaining quality unrefined components at cutthroat costs. Besides, they frequently need bartering power with providers, which can bring about ominous inventory terms. Further developing inventory network the executives, building provider connections, and investigating mass buying choices can assist with relieving these difficulties.

The absence of economies of scale is another test that limited scale ventures should fight with. Because of their restricted creation limit, they might battle to accomplish cost efficiencies delighted in by bigger undertakings. This can make their items more costly, making it trying to contend on the lookout. Cooperative game plans, like group advancement and agreeable showcasing, can empower limited scope enterprises to pool assets and upgrade their seriousness.

Energy costs and ecological manageability are additionally squeezing concerns. Limited scope enterprises are many times energy-escalated, and fluctuating energy costs can altogether influence their functional expenses. Furthermore, they might not have the assets to take on manageable and eco-accommodating practices, which can prompt natural debasement. Government motivators for taking on energy-effective advancements and manageable practices can assist with tending to these difficulties.

Admittance to data and innovation is difficult for limited scope ventures. In the time of advanced change, approaching applicable data and innovation is imperative for remaining cutthroat. Some limited scale business people miss the mark on information and assets to saddle the force of advanced devices and internet business.

Giving preparation and admittance to data and correspondence innovation can connect this advanced gap and enable limited scope organizations.

Unstable economic situations and monetary unsteadiness can be especially negative to limited scope enterprises. These organizations frequently come up short on monetary pad to climate financial slumps, and their endurance can be undermined during seasons of downturn or market choppiness. Creating flexibility through monetary preparation, expansion, and hazard the board techniques is fundamental to explore these vulnerabilities.

Globalization presents the two valuable open doors and difficulties for limited scope enterprises. While it gives admittance to worldwide business sectors and potential open doors for development, it additionally opens these organizations to expanded contest from worldwide players. Exploring the intricacies of global exchange, incorporating consistence with worldwide guidelines and managing conversion standard vacillations, can be overwhelming for limited scope endeavors.

Admittance to gifted administrative ability is another test that limited scale ventures face. Numerous business visionaries might have brilliant specialized abilities however come up short on administrative mastery expected to effectively maintain a business. Creating the executives abilities and cultivating a culture of consistent learning can assist with beating this obstacle.

Limited scope ventures in provincial regions frequently face exceptional difficulties connected with framework, network, and admittance to assets. The metropolitan rustic separation can worsen these difficulties, making it challenging for provincial ventures to contend and flourish. Government arrangements that advance rustic turn of events and give motivations to provincial organizations can assist with tending to these abberations.

Deficient admittance to credit and monetary administrations is a test that merits unique consideration. Limited scope ventures, particularly those in the casual area, frequently work outside the formal monetary framework. This restricts their admittance to credit, protection, and other monetary administrations. Advancing monetary incorporation and creating microfinance foundations custom-made to the necessities of limited scope business people can work on their monetary strength and flexibility.

Protected innovation privileges and innovation move can likewise be quite difficult for limited scope ventures. These organizations might come up short on assets and mastery to safeguard their licensed innovation, which can bring about the deficiency of important developments. Working with the most common way of licensing and safeguarding licensed innovation can empower advancement and intensity among limited scope endeavors.

In numerous nations, defilement and regulatory administrative noise present critical difficulties for limited scope enterprises. Business visionaries frequently experience requests for pay-offs, defers in endorsements, and other degenerate practices that can build the expense of carrying on with work and block development.

Executing straightforwardness measures, smoothing out regulatory cycles, and genuinely honest encouraging a culture can assist with handling this issue.

Limited scope businesses working in areas like agribusiness frequently face erratic atmospheric conditions and environmental change-related difficulties. These organizations are profoundly subject to normal assets, and any disturbance in weather conditions can affect their efficiency and benefit. Empowering maintainable horticultural practices and giving admittance to environment versatile advances can help with moderating the impacts of environmental change.

Admittance to innovation and development is a test that limited scale enterprises should address to remain serious in the cutting edge business scene. Quick mechanical headways can possibly change businesses, and limited scope ventures that don't embrace these progressions might end up in a difficult situation. Interest in innovative work, innovation dispersion, and development backing can assist these organizations with remaining pertinent and cutthroat.

Social and social variables can likewise present difficulties to limited scope enterprises. At times, customary cultural standards and social practices might thwart the cooperation of specific gatherings, like ladies or underestimated networks, in pioneering exercises. Advancing orientation balance, variety, and consideration can assist with defeating these hindrances and tap into the enterprising capability of all fragments of society.

Market vacillations and request vulnerabilities can fundamentally influence limited scope ventures. These organizations might battle to anticipate and answer changes in purchaser inclinations and market elements. Creating market knowledge, broadening item contributions, and upgrading advertising methodologies can assist limited scope enterprises with adjusting to changing economic situations.

5.1 Access to Capital and Resources

Admittance to capital and assets is an essential test that significantly affects the development and supportability of organizations, particularly for limited scope endeavors. This challenge envelops a few perspectives, including monetary capital, actual assets, innovation, and HR. In this conversation, we will investigate the basic job of admittance to capital and assets, the difficulties limited scope organizations face in such manner, and expected answers for beat these hindrances.

Monetary Capital

Monetary capital is the backbone of any business. It is fundamental for beginning, working, and growing a business. Limited scope endeavors frequently face hardships in getting to sufficient monetary capital. Customary banks and monetary organizations might be reluctant to loan to these organizations because of their apparent higher gamble. Also, rigid guarantee necessities can make it trying for little business visionaries to get advances. This absence of admittance to monetary capital can block business development and cutoff the capability of limited scope endeavors.

Some limited scale business visionaries resort to casual wellsprings of money, like moneylenders and unregulated microfinance foundations, to meet their capital necessities. While these sources can give transient help, they frequently accompany extravagant loan fees, prompting a pattern of obligation and monetary precariousness. Resolving the issue of monetary capital is significant for limited scope organizations to put resources into hardware, foundation, and working capital, as well as to endure financial slumps and immediately take advantage of development chances.

To further develop admittance to monetary capital, state run administrations, monetary foundations, and improvement associations can go to a few lengths. One methodology is to make specific loaning programs and monetary items custom-made to the requirements of limited scope ventures. These projects can offer positive terms, lower loan fees, and diminished security prerequisites. Moreover, monetary proficiency and business venture preparing can engage little business visionaries to settle on informed monetary choices and explore the complicated universe of money really.

Notwithstanding conventional monetary foundations, shared loaning stages and crowdfunding have arisen as elective wellsprings of subsidizing for limited scope organizations. These imaginative methodologies can interface business visionaries with individual financial backers ready to give funding to promising endeavors. Legislatures and associations can support the development of these stages and guarantee they work inside an administrative system to safeguard the two moneylenders and borrowers.

Actual Assets

Admittance to actual assets, like land, foundation, and utilities, is urgent for limited scope endeavors. Nonetheless, these assets are in many cases restricted and might be inconsistent conveyed. Rustic regions, specifically, face difficulties connected with foundation and availability. Deficient transportation, absence of power, and questionable water supply can upset creation and increment functional expenses for organizations around there.

States and improvement organizations can assume a significant part in further developing admittance to actual assets. Putting resources into country framework, like streets, power lattices, and water supply frameworks, can help limited scope ventures as well as the general improvement of provincial networks. Public-private associations can likewise assist with crossing over the asset hole by empowering private area interests in framework advancement.

Land residency issues can be a critical obstacle for limited scope organizations, particularly in emerging nations. Absence of clear land proprietorship freedoms can prevent business visionaries from putting resources into land and land. Legitimate changes, property privileges enlistment frameworks, and straightforward land obtaining cycles can resolve these issues and furnish limited scope endeavors with the certainty to put resources into land-based adventures.

Admittance to innovation is one more part of actual assets that can fundamentally affect limited scope organizations. Obsolete hardware and innovation can block efficiency and seriousness. Little business visionaries might not have the assets to redesign their innovation, making them less cutthroat on the lookout. Giving admittance to present day innovation and working with innovation move can assist limited scope ventures with working on their effectiveness and item quality.

HR

Admittance to talented and inspired HR is a basic part of business achievement. Nonetheless, limited scope organizations frequently battle to find and hold qualified workers. Numerous gifted laborers favor the professional stability and advantages presented by bigger partnerships, making it trying for little endeavors to draw in top ability.

Moreover, limited scope organizations might not have the assets to put resources into preparing and improvement programs for their representatives. This can bring about ability holes and decreased efficiency. To resolve the issue of HR, little business people can take on a few systems. Offering serious wages and advantages can make limited scope endeavors more alluring to expected representatives. Besides, establishing a favorable workplace that stresses expertise improvement and professional success can assist with holding gifted specialists.

In locales with an overflow of work however restricted open doors, limited scope ventures can act as a wellspring of business. Nonetheless, business people frequently experience hardships in tracking down appropriate work. To overcome this issue, state run administrations can uphold ability advancement programs, professional preparation, and apprenticeship drives. These actions can outfit laborers with the abilities expected to fulfill the needs of limited scope endeavors and give them the valuable chance to get better work.

Besides, advancing business venture training can sustain a culture of development and independent work among the young, empowering them to become business visionaries and make their organizations. These endeavors can assist with tending to the human asset challenges looked by limited scope businesses and engage them to develop and succeed.

Market Access

Admittance to business sectors is basic for limited scope undertakings to sell their items and administrations. Notwithstanding, they frequently face difficulties in advertising and dissemination, which can restrict their span and likely deals. Little business people might come up short on assets and information to showcase their items really, leaving them in a difficult spot in the cutthroat business scene.

Government and industry affiliations can help limited scope ventures in creating powerful advertising and appropriation procedures. Giving preparation and mentorship in promoting, marking, and deals can assist business people with improving their market presence and draw in clients. Also, building solid dispersion organizations, whether through associations or online business stages, can expand the market access for limited scope organizations.

Market data is one more basic part of market access. Little business people might battle to remain informed about changing customer inclinations and market patterns. To address this, state run administrations and industry associations can give market knowledge and examination administrations to limited scope undertakings. This data outfits business visionaries with the information expected to adjust to changing economic situations and pursue informed business choices.

Worldwide business sectors present the two amazing open doors and difficulties for limited scope enterprises. While worldwide business sectors offer potential for development and expansion, they likewise open these organizations to serious worldwide contest. Admittance to unfamiliar business sectors can be confined by profession obstructions, absence of market data, and complex product methodology.

To assist limited scope endeavors with exploring the intricacies of global exchange, states can offer help in exchange help and product advancement. This can incorporate smoothing out send out strategies, lessening duties, and giving exchange money and protection choices. Besides, improving admittance to exchange data and commodity advancement projects can engage little business visionaries to investigate worldwide business sectors and contend really.

Inventory network The executives

Limited scope undertakings frequently face difficulties connected with inventory network the executives. Obtaining quality unrefined substances at serious costs can be troublesome, and they might not have the haggling power with providers delighted in by bigger organizations. Little business people may likewise come up short on assets to put resources into complex inventory network the executives frameworks.

Effective store network the executives is fundamental for diminishing functional expenses and guaranteeing ideal conveyance of unrefined substances and completed items. To address these difficulties, limited scope organizations can investigate choices, for example, building solid associations with providers, taking part in bunch buying plans, and streamlining stock administration processes. These methodologies can assist little business people with further developing their production network proficiency and cost-adequacy.

Additionally, computerized advancements and online business stages can upgrade production network perceivability and coordination. Carrying out production network the board programming and taking on internet business arrangements can assist limited scope undertakings with smoothing out their acquisition and appropriation processes, diminishing expenses and further developing responsiveness to showcase requests.

Energy Expenses and Natural Manageability

The expense and accessibility of energy are huge difficulties for limited scope enterprises. Fluctuating energy costs and temperamental stockpile can influence functional expenses and productivity. Besides, limited scope organizations might not have the assets to put resources into energy-productive innovations, making them more powerless against rising energy costs.

5.2 Marketing and Competition

Promoting and contest are two interconnected mainstays of business that assume a fundamental part in the achievement and maintainability of any venture, including limited scope organizations. This conversation digs into the significance of promoting and the difficulties looked by limited scope enterprises in this domain, as well as procedures to actually explore contest in the present powerful business scene.

Advertising's Pivotal Job

Promoting is something beyond a bunch of exercises pointed toward selling items or administrations; it is the foundation of building a brand, making client mindfulness, and laying out a dedicated client base. Powerful advertising is the key part for limited scope organizations to make due and flourish in an undeniably aggressive worldwide commercial center.

Nonetheless, limited scope ventures frequently wrestle with restricted assets, making it trying to devise and execute exhaustive showcasing techniques. These organizations might come up short on skill, spending plans, and framework expected to take part in customary publicizing and promoting efforts. Therefore, they face special difficulties in showcasing their items or administrations actually.

Challenges in Showcasing

Restricted Financial plans: Limited scope undertakings regularly work with compelled financial plans. Designating assets to showcasing endeavors can be an overwhelming undertaking, especially when other functional costs request quick consideration. This monetary limit can hinder the production of convincing promoting materials, missions, and methodologies.

Absence of Ability: Numerous little business visionaries have specialized abilities connected with their items or administrations however may need mastery in advertising. Creating a successful promoting methodology, figuring out purchaser conduct, and planning convincing publicizing efforts frequently require particular information and experience.

Insufficient Framework: Foundation, both physical and computerized, is fundamental for viable promoting. Limited scope organizations might miss the mark on important framework to help web based showcasing, internet business stages, or complex client relationship the executives frameworks. Insufficient foundation can prevent their promoting endeavors and responsiveness to client requests.

Admittance to Market Data: Limited scope organizations might battle to get to pertinent market data and shopper experiences. Without admittance to such information, they find it trying to adjust to changing economic situations, meet customer inclinations, and settle on informed promoting choices.

Restricted Appropriation Organizations: Many little endeavors depend on customary dispersion channels, which might have restricted reach. Growing conveyance organizations can be trying because of asset limitations and the intricacies of laying out associations with wholesalers and retailers.

Powerful Systems to Beat Promoting Difficulties

Advanced Showcasing: In the computerized age, limited scope organizations can bridle the force of web based promoting. Computerized promoting techniques, for example, web-based entertainment publicizing, site improvement (Search engine optimization), and email showcasing, offer financially savvy ways of contacting a more extensive crowd. These systems are open and can yield quantifiable outcomes.

Content Promoting: Content advertising, including writing for a blog, video content, and infographics, can lay out private companies as experts in their specialty. Making significant, useful substance can draw in and connect with clients while building memorability.

Systems administration and Associations: Working together with different organizations, industry affiliations, or neighborhood networks can grow the promoting reach of limited scope endeavors. Organizing gives valuable chances to cross-advancement, joint endeavors, and shared help in showcasing endeavors.

Client Relationship The board (CRM) Frameworks: Carrying out CRM frameworks can assist private ventures with overseeing client information, track associations, and designer advertising endeavors to individual client inclinations. CRM programming can improve client commitment and reliability.

Statistical surveying: Leading statistical surveying, even on a limited scale, can give important experiences into purchaser conduct and inclinations. Gathering information through overviews, center gatherings, or online examination can illuminate advertising techniques and item improvement.

Client Tributes and Audits: Empowering fulfilled clients to leave tributes and surveys can assemble trust and validity. Positive input from existing clients can act as powerful showcasing materials.

Rivalry in the Cutting edge Scene

Rivalry in the business world has become progressively unique and complex, with new players entering the market and laid out organizations continually advancing to keep up with their strategic advantage. Limited scope ventures face a few special difficulties connected with contest that can influence their development and maintainability.

Challenges in Contest

Restricted Assets: Limited scope endeavors frequently work with restricted assets contrasted with bigger organizations. This asset imperative can put them in a difficult situation with regards to showcasing, innovative work, and size of tasks.

Extreme Contention: Private ventures might end up in exceptionally serious business sectors where various players compete for a similar client base. This serious contention can prompt cost wars, lessening net revenues and restricting the ability to put resources into development and advancement.

Portion of the overall industry: Acquiring and keeping up with piece of the pie can be quite difficult for limited scope ventures. They frequently face rivalry from bigger organizations with laid out brands and broad appropriation organizations. These bigger contenders might utilize their market ability to extract more modest players from the market.

Innovation and Development: Staying aware of mechanical progressions and advancements can be challenging for limited scope organizations. Bigger companies might have the assets to put resources into state of the art innovations and innovative work, making it trying for more modest ventures to contend on a similar mechanical balance.

Administrative Hindrances: Limited scope enterprises might experience administrative boundaries that favor bigger companies. These guidelines can force consistence expenses and breaking point market access for more modest players.

Successful Procedures to Conquer Contest Difficulties

Specialty Situating: Limited scope undertakings can cut out a specialty for themselves by zeroing in on a particular fragment of the market. Specialty situating permits organizations to take care of a more designated crowd and contend successfully by offering specific items or administrations.

Client Driven Approach: Focusing on extraordinary client support and building solid associations with clients can separate independent ventures from bigger contenders. Customized administration and regard for client necessities can prompt client unwaveringness.

Advancement and Variation: Limited scope enterprises ought to embrace development and adjust to changing economic situations. Recognizing arising patterns, innovations, and client inclinations can give an upper hand.

Vital Associations: Teaming up with different organizations or going into key organizations can extend the compass and capacities of limited scope endeavors. Banding together with correlative organizations can give chances to joint promoting endeavors and the sharing of assets.

Cost Effectiveness: Keeping up with cost productivity is fundamental for limited scope businesses to stay cutthroat. Smoothing out tasks, streamlining supply chains, and decreasing above costs can assist private companies with offering serious costs and further develop net revenues.

Legitimate and Administrative Promotion: Limited scope enterprises can advocate for fair and evenhanded guidelines and arrangements. Joining industry affiliations and taking part in support endeavors can assist with evening the odds and lessen administrative boundaries.

Nonstop Mastering and Expertise Improvement: Empowering representatives to constantly refresh their abilities and information can upgrade an organization's capacity to successfully contend. Giving preparation and advancement amazing open doors can engage workers to add to the organization's development.

Limited scope businesses that influence powerful advertising and contest procedures can make due as well as flourish even with difficulties. These techniques permit them to expand their assets and defeat their restrictions, empowering them to lay out a traction in serious business sectors. Moreover, the versatility, advancement, and client focal point of limited scope ventures can be significant resources in exploring the present consistently developing business scene.

5.3 Regulation and Compliance

Guideline and consistence are indispensable parts of any business climate, no matter what its size or industry. They give a structure to guaranteeing fair rivalry, safeguarding shoppers, and advancing the general soundness of the market. Limited scope ventures, similar to their bigger partners, should explore an intricate trap of rules and guidelines. In this conversation, we will investigate the meaning of guideline and consistence, the difficulties looked by limited scope enterprises in gathering these necessities, and likely procedures to upgrade administrative consistence.

The Meaning of Guideline and Consistence

Guideline and consistence serve a few basic capabilities in the business scene:

Buyer Security: Guidelines frequently incorporate arrangements intended to shield purchasers from unreasonable strategic approaches, hazardous items, and fake showcasing. These assurances are essential for keeping up with trust and trust on the lookout.

Market Steadiness: Guidelines assist with keeping up with market solidness by forestalling misrepresentation, out of line rivalry, and monopolistic practices. They set the guidelines of the game, guaranteeing that organizations work inside a fair and serious climate.

Ecological and Moral Norms: Guidelines might incorporate natural and moral principles that organizations should comply with. These norms are fundamental for advancing maintainability, lessening negative externalities, and maintaining cultural qualities.

General Wellbeing and Security: Numerous guidelines are set up to defend general wellbeing and wellbeing. This can incorporate sanitation guidelines, working environment security guidelines, and item quality control measures.

Challenges in Administrative Consistence

Limited scope ventures frequently face a huge number of difficulties with regards to administrative consistence. These difficulties can be both down to earth and monetary, making it more hard for them to really explore the administrative scene:

Intricacy of Guidelines: Guidelines can be perplexing and likely to visit changes. Limited scope undertakings might miss the mark on assets or ability to keep awake to date with developing guidelines and their suggestions.

Monetary Limitations: Consistence with guidelines can be exorbitant. Independent ventures might battle to allot the vital assets for consistence, which can prevent their development and functional limit.

Absence of Mastery: Understanding and deciphering guidelines is a particular expertise. Limited scope organizations might not have committed consistence officials or lawful groups, making it trying with guarantee that they are complying to all important principles.

Regulatory Weight: The managerial weight of conforming to guidelines, including record-keeping, revealing, and documentation, can be overpowering for limited scope ventures with restricted staff and assets.

Lawful Results: Rebelliousness can prompt legitimate outcomes, including fines and punishments. For private companies, these punishments can be especially oppressive and possibly pulverizing.

Techniques to Improve Administrative Consistence

While the difficulties of administrative consistence are critical, there are methodologies that limited scale enterprises can embrace to upgrade their capacity to successfully meet administrative necessities:

Draw in with Administrative Specialists: Building a helpful connection with administrative specialists can furnish private companies with knowledge and direction. Customary correspondence and criticism can assist them with grasping the subtleties of guidelines and exhibit their obligation to consistence.

Preparing and Schooling: Putting resources into preparing and training for representatives on administrative issues is vital. This enables staff to recognize consistence issues, keep up with records, and guarantee that the business works inside the limits of the law.

Consistence Programming: Using consistence programming and innovation can smooth out authoritative undertakings connected with administrative consistence. These devices can help limited scope endeavors track and oversee consistence necessities all the more productively.

Re-appropriating Consistence Capabilities: Independent ventures can consider re-appropriating explicit consistence capabilities to outer specialists or advisors. This can be a practical method for guaranteeing that all administrative viewpoints are overseen really.

Coordinated effort and Data Sharing: Working together with industry affiliations and companion associations can be valuable. These organizations can give potential chances to share data and best works on in regards to administrative consistence.

Focus on Consistence in Business Arranging: Limited scope organizations ought to implant administrative consistence into their field-tested strategies and methodologies. This proactive methodology guarantees that consistence isn't a reconsideration however a basic part of tasks.

Standard Reviews and Self-Appraisal: Leading normal inner reviews and self-evaluation can assist organizations with distinguishing potential consistence holes and correct them before they become significant issues.

Access Monetary Assets: To address monetary limitations, private companies can investigate choices, for example, government awards, sponsorships, and monetary impetuses intended to help consistence endeavors.

Remain Informed and Partake in Backing: Staying up with the latest with administrative changes and taking part in industry-explicit support endeavors can guarantee that organizations have a voice in molding guidelines that influence them.

The Job of Government and Controllers

Notwithstanding the endeavors of limited scope enterprises, states and administrative bodies likewise play a urgent part to play in working with administrative consistence for private companies. These elements can execute measures to help limited scope ventures in their consistence endeavors:

Worked on Guidelines: Legislatures can endeavor to improve on guidelines and make them more open to private companies. Clear and direct guidelines are simpler for limited scope ventures with comprehend and comply to.

Consistence Help Projects: Legislatures can lay out consistence help programs custom fitted to the necessities of private companies. These projects can give preparing, assets, and backing to improve consistence endeavors.

Administrative Help: Giving administrative help to limited scope businesses through decreased charges, smoothed out announcing, or exceptions can ease the monetary weight of consistence.

Monetary Help: Legislatures can offer monetary help, including awards and low-premium advances, to assist private ventures with putting resources into consistence measures.

Public Mindfulness Missions: Sending off open mindfulness missions can assist with teaching independent ventures about the significance of consistence and the assets accessible to help their endeavors.

One-Stop Administrative Focuses: Laying out one-stop administrative focuses where independent ventures can get to data, direction, and help on different consistence matters can work on the interaction.

Impetuses for Economical Works on: Giving motivators to embracing feasible and naturally capable practices can persuade limited scope enterprises to agree with ecological guidelines.

Adaptability in Implementation: Administrative specialists can practice adaptability in authorization, especially for minor or accidental infringement, by giving alerts and open doors to restorative activity.

The Eventual fate of Guideline and Consistence

The administrative scene is constantly developing, formed by elements like innovative headways, changing purchaser assumptions, and arising gambles. For limited scope businesses, remaining educated and versatile is fundamental for meet developing consistence necessities.

Digitalization and Innovation: As innovation keeps on progressing, administrative consistence is progressively turning into a computerized try. Limited scope undertakings ought to put resources into consistence programming, information safety efforts, and network safety with safeguard delicate data and comply to information protection guidelines.

Ecological Maintainability: Supportability and natural guidelines are turning out to be more unmistakable. Private companies ought to coordinate eco-accommodating practices into their tasks, which guarantees consistence as well as requests to naturally cognizant purchasers.

Purchaser Security and Information Insurance: With developing worries about information security, consistence with guidelines like the Overall Information Assurance Guideline (GDPR) is fundamental. Limited scope businesses taking care of client information ought to focus on consistence and information security measures.

Globalization: Private companies hoping to extend universally should know about worldwide guidelines. Worldwide exchange and product import consistence might turn out to be progressively significant for limited scope enterprises with worldwide aspirations.

Flexibility: Independent ventures ought to stay coordinated and ready to adjust to new administrative necessities. Ordinary evaluations of consistence techniques and proactive endeavors to line up with advancing guidelines are significant.

Chapter 6

Support Mechanisms and Initiatives

In our quickly impacting world, support systems and drives assume a urgent part in sustaining development and prosperity for people and networks. These systems and drives come in different structures, tending to assorted needs and difficulties that individuals face in various circles of life. From schooling to medical care, from monetary security to social incorporation, the job of help systems and drives couldn't possibly be more significant. This exposition digs into the meaning of these systems and drives, investigating their effect on private and aggregate prosperity.

One of the key mainstays of help instruments is instruction. Training has been and stays a vital determinant of individual and cultural turn of events. Admittance to quality instruction has the ability to change lives, outfitting people with the information and abilities expected to accomplish their maximum capacity. Lately, there has been a developing acknowledgment of the significance of comprehensive schooling, where support components are laid out to take care of different students, incorporating those with inabilities. This shift towards inclusivity not just upgrades the prosperity of minimized people yet additionally enhances the generally speaking instructive experience, advancing resistance and understanding among the more extensive understudy body.

Support components in schooling reach out past inclusivity. Grants, awards, and monetary guide programs are significant drives that empower people, independent of their financial foundations, to get to advanced education. These components make everything fair, guaranteeing that ability and assurance, instead of monetary means, become the essential determinants of progress. Besides, tutoring and vocation direction programs offer priceless help for understudies in settling on informed decisions about their future, hence adding to their drawn out prosperity.

In the domain of medical services, support systems and drives are similarly imperative. Admittance to quality medical services is an essential common liberty, and backing systems are expected to guarantee that this right is maintained. Public medical care frameworks, supported by legislatures, are one of the most well-known and powerful method for giving medical services admittance to all residents, no matter what their pay. These frameworks are supported by drives, for example, general medical care, which guarantees that fundamental clinical benefits are accessible to everybody without monetary boundaries. Such components advance actual prosperity as well as add to monetary prosperity by decreasing the monetary weight of medical care on people and families.

Past open medical services, support systems and drives are crucial in tending to explicit wellbeing challenges. For example, the ascent of ongoing sicknesses lately has prompted the improvement of preventive wellbeing projects and drives. These drives plan to instruct and enable people to pursue solid way of life decisions, eventually lessening the pervasiveness of preventable sicknesses. Furthermore, psychological wellbeing support components have acquired conspicuousness as social orders perceive the significance of mental prosperity. Drives like emergency hotlines, treatment administrations, and destigmatization endeavors have taken huge steps in offering the fundamental help for people confronting emotional wellness challenges.

Monetary solidness is one more basic part of prosperity, and backing systems and drives in this area have extensive impacts. Joblessness can be a significant wellspring of stress and frailty for people and families. In that capacity, joblessness advantages and occupation preparing programs act as significant help systems, offering a monetary security net while outfitting people with the abilities expected to reemerge the labor force. Even with monetary shocks, social security nets like food help projects and lodging sponsorships assume a fundamental part in keeping individuals from falling into neediness, guaranteeing their general prosperity stays in one piece.

Business and independent company improvement drives additionally add to monetary prosperity. These help instruments engage people to set out their own monetary open doors, encouraging advancement and financial development. Hatcheries, awards, and business mentorship programs are only a couple of instances of drives that furnish hopeful business people with the instruments and direction they need to succeed, subsequently supporting financial prosperity at both the individual and local area levels.

In the domain of social consideration, support systems and drives are fundamental for making a general public where everybody feels esteemed and has an equivalent chance to flourish. Variety and consideration programs in the working environment are an illustration of such drives. These projects advance a more fair and agreeable workplace, where people from different foundations are urged to contribute their special points of view. This upgrades the prosperity of workers as well as fortifies the association by encouraging imagination and advancement.

Support systems for minimized and weak populaces, like exiles and outsiders, are essential in guaranteeing social consideration. Resettlement programs, language classes, and social reconciliation drives assist rookies with adjusting to their new social orders and construct a feeling of having a place. Such help instruments are philanthropic as well as fundamental for social union and security.

Local area based drives assume a basic part in supporting social prosperity. Charitable associations, public venues, and grassroots developments are instances of these components.

They frequently address explicit nearby difficulties, for example, destitution, substance misuse, or wrongdoing. By giving assets, administrations, and a feeling of local area, these drives assist with further developing the general prosperity of the people they serve, adding to the improvement of the whole local area.

Ecological prosperity is a component of help instruments and drives that has acquired noticeable quality as the world wrestles with natural difficulties. Environmental change, contamination, and asset consumption are compromising the prosperity of current and people in the future. Support components in this area incorporate ecological assurance strategies and drives that mean to relieve these difficulties. Instances of such drives are environmentally friendly power advancement, protection endeavors, and supportability programs that empower mindful asset the board. By defending the climate, these components add to the drawn out prosperity of the planet and its occupants.

Emergency reaction and fiasco the board are one more essential part of help components. Catastrophic events, pandemics, and clashes can have annihilating ramifications for people and networks. Government and non-legislative associations frequently lay out catastrophe alleviation and emergency reaction drives to give quick guide, haven, and medical care to those impacted. These drives are a life saver for people confronting such emergencies and are instrumental in reestablishing a feeling of safety and prosperity.

In the computerized age, innovation and the web have opened up new roads for help systems and drives. Online people group and care groups have arisen as wellsprings of profound and educational help for people confronting different difficulties. These virtual stages make spaces for individuals to associate, share encounters, and access assets that add to their prosperity. Additionally, telemedicine and teletherapy have become progressively available, giving distant medical services and emotional well-being support, especially in underserved or far off regions.

With regards to the worldwide local area, global guide and improvement help are fundamental help systems for nations confronting financial, social, or natural difficulties. Unfamiliar guide, compassionate help, and advancement programs assist countries with building framework, further develop medical services and training, and address destitution and disparity. These drives assume a huge part in advancing worldwide dependability and prosperity by lifting whole populaces out of destitution and supporting their drawn out improvement.

In any case, it is critical to perceive that help systems and drives are not without their difficulties and impediments. One significant issue is financing and asset designation. Many help programs depend on government financing, and spending plan imperatives can restrict the degree and adequacy of these drives. Lacking subsidizing can bring about lengthy hanging tight records for fundamental administrations, decreased program quality, and biased admittance to help components. States must focus on the designation of assets to guarantee that help drives are enough supported and open to those out of luck.

Another test is the potential for help components to make reliance accidentally. While these systems are intended to enable people and networks, there is a gamble that certain individuals might become dependent on the help and not effectively pursue independence. Finding some kind of harmony between giving fundamental help and empowering confidence is a complicated errand that help programs should address.

Additionally, support instruments and drives can be helpless against political and philosophical movements. Changes in government initiative and strategy bearing can influence the financing and course of these drives, possibly leaving the people who depend on them in a condition of vulnerability. Long haul arranging and bipartisan help for key help components are important to guarantee their security and adequacy.

Now and again, support instruments may coincidentally sustain fundamental imbalances. For instance, governmental policy regarding minorities in society programs intended to advance variety in training and work can confront analysis for turn around segregation.

6.1 Government Policies and Incentives

Government strategies and motivating forces assume an essential part in shaping social orders and economies all over the planet. These actions, frequently determined by a blend of political, social, and monetary contemplations, are fundamental devices for legislatures to seek after their objectives and address the intricate difficulties of the cutting edge period. Whether they relate to medical care, schooling, the climate, or the economy, government strategies and motivators significantly affect the existences of people and the improvement of countries. This exposition investigates the different manners by which government arrangements and motivations impact our reality.

One of the principal regions where government strategies have a critical effect is medical services. Admittance to quality medical services is a foundation of prosperity and cultural turn of events. States all over the planet have created medical services arrangements pointed toward guaranteeing that their residents can get fundamental clinical consideration. General medical care frameworks, where the public authority gives medical care administrations to all occupants, are a perfect representation. Such frameworks guarantee that medical care isn't restricted to the individuals who can manage the cost of it, elevating fair admittance to fundamental administrations and further developing general wellbeing results.

Impetuses in medical care strategies likewise assume a basic part. For example, states might offer duty motivations to people who buy health care coverage, in this way uplifting a more extensive populace to get inclusion. Also, innovative work impetuses are utilized to advance development in the medical care area. These impetuses can appear as awards or tax reductions for drug organizations and clinical gadget producers, empowering them to put resources into new medicines and innovations that benefit society overall.

Schooling is one more domain profoundly affected by government approaches and motivators. Admittance to quality training is a principal right and a critical driver of cultural advancement. State run administrations are liable for creating arrangements that guarantee fair admittance to schooling for all residents. For example, obligatory training regulations command that kids go to class, advancing broad education and information obtaining. Monetary help components, like grants and awards, urge understudies to seek after advanced education, no matter what their financial foundations.

Motivating forces in training arrangements are intended to work on the nature of schooling and empower the improvement of basic abilities. Instructor preparing projects and expert improvement impetuses assist with making a gifted and spurred educating labor force. Research motivations support instructive exploration and advancement, prompting the improvement of viable showing strategies and instructive innovations. These motivating forces add to the constant improvement of the school system and the prosperity of the people it serves.

Monetary arrangements, both at the public and worldwide levels, are instrumental in molding the success and soundness of social orders. States execute financial and money related arrangements to direct monetary exercises, control expansion, and invigorate monetary development. Tax collection approaches, for instance, can fundamentally influence the appropriation of abundance and pay. Moderate duty frameworks, where higher-pay people pay a more noteworthy extent of their pay in charges, are utilized to diminish pay imbalance and asset fundamental taxpayer supported organizations.

Motivators inside financial approaches are intended to animate explicit monetary exercises. Speculation tax reductions urge organizations to put resources into capital gear and extend their tasks. These motivations encourage monetary development as well as add to work creation and worked on expectations for everyday comforts. Exchange strategies, including duties and import/trade motivators, are utilized to advance or safeguard homegrown enterprises, influencing the generally financial well-being of a country.

Natural approaches and motivators are progressively essential as the world appearances squeezing biological difficulties. Government strategies are urgent in directing and moderating the effects of environmental change, contamination, and asset exhaustion. Drives, for example, carbon evaluating, through carbon charges or cap-and-exchange frameworks, give impetuses to people and organizations to diminish their ozone harming substance emanations. These motivations assist with combatting environmental change by adjusting monetary interests to natural objectives.

Motivations in natural arrangements can appear as appropriations for sustainable power creation or tax breaks for the acquisition of electric vehicles. Such motivating forces drive development and speed up the change to a more manageable economy.

Also, protection approaches, including safeguarded regions and natural life conservation motivating forces, mean to defend biodiversity and biological systems. These arrangements add to the prosperity of current and people in the future by guaranteeing the wellbeing of the normal world.

Social strategies address a great many cultural difficulties, including neediness, joblessness, and social imbalance. Government help programs, for example, government assistance and joblessness benefits, offer monetary help to people and families out of luck. These strategies are fundamental wellbeing nets that keep weak populaces from falling into neediness and offer fundamental help during seasons of financial difficulty.

Motivating forces inside friendly arrangements advance wanted ways of behaving and results. Acquired personal tax reductions, for instance, urge low-pay people to work by furnishing charge discounts that increment with procured pay. Childcare sponsorships and parental leave motivators support working guardians by lessening the monetary weight of childcare and taking into consideration balance between serious and fun activities. These motivators add to individual and family prosperity and by and large friendly soundness.

Work strategies assume a huge part in molding the working environment and the states of business. The lowest pay permitted by law regulations, for instance, lay out a benchmark pay level for laborers, guaranteeing that they procure a fair compensation for their work. Work environment security guidelines and motivating forces urge bosses to give safe working circumstances, safeguarding the wellbeing and prosperity of representatives.

Motivators in labor strategies may likewise incorporate work preparing and apprenticeship programs that outfit laborers with the abilities expected to prevail in the advanced work market. These drives support profession improvement, upgrade employability, and eventually add to the general prosperity of the labor force.

Unfamiliar and worldwide strategies are vital to a country's commitment with the worldwide local area. State run administrations utilize international strategies to lay out political relations, arrange settlements, and oversee global contentions. Worldwide advancement impetuses, for example, unfamiliar guide and specialized help programs, plan to help different countries in their endeavors to ease neediness, further develop medical services, and address ecological difficulties.

Exchange approaches, frequently some portion of unfamiliar and worldwide techniques, can have expansive financial effects. State run administrations arrange economic accords and deal exchange motivations to advance the trading of labor and products between countries. These motivations work with monetary development and set out open doors for organizations and laborers, upgrading worldwide thriving.

Public safety and guard strategies are fundamental for shielding a country's sway and the prosperity of its residents. States assign assets to fabricate and keep up with military, foster guard procedures, and lay out global partnerships. Motivators inside these arrangements might incorporate military enlistment impetuses, support for veterans, and safeguard innovative work financing. These motivations are critical for guaranteeing public safety and the assurance of residents.

While government approaches and motivations are useful assets for shaping social orders and economies, they are not without their difficulties and restrictions. Strategy plan and execution can be impacted by political contemplations, prompting momentary direction and hardliner gridlock. Compelling arrangements require insightful preparation, long haul vision, and bipartisan help to resolve complicated and getting through issues.

Adjusting contending interests and needs is a consistent test in strategy making. For instance, arrangements that plan to animate monetary development and occupation creation may unintentionally prompt natural debasement. Finding some kind of harmony among financial and natural targets is a mind boggling task that legislatures should address.

Straightforwardness and responsibility are basic parts of powerful government approaches. Residents reserve the option to know how approaches are figured out and executed and ought to possess the ability to consider their state run administrations responsible for their activities. An absence of straightforwardness and responsibility can prompt defilement, failure, and the abuse of public assets.

The potentially negative side-effects of strategies and impetuses can likewise present difficulties. For example, good natured sponsorships for explicit enterprises might contort market rivalry, make shortcomings, and lead to financial disparities. Cautious assessment and constant checking of strategies are important to distinguish and address accidental unfortunate results.

The worldwide interconnectedness of social orders and economies implies that administration approaches and motivations frequently have global ramifications. Exchange approaches, natural guidelines, and unfamiliar guide projects can influence different countries and worldwide frameworks. Facilitated global endeavors and tact are expected to address normal difficulties, for example, environmental change, psychological oppression, and general wellbeing emergencies.

6.2 Microfinance and Loan Programs

Microfinance and credit programs are extraordinary instruments for enabling people, networks, and independent ventures all over the planet. These drives give admittance to monetary assets and administrations, empowering individuals to defeat financial difficulties, work on their vocations, and departure the pattern of neediness. In this exposition, we will investigate the meaning of microfinance and credit programs, their effect on neediness decrease, and the difficulties and amazing open doors they present.

Microfinance is a monetary help area that spotlights on giving little credits, bank accounts, and other monetary items to people and independent companies who have restricted admittance to conventional financial administrations. The idea of microfinance acquired conspicuousness in the late twentieth 100 years, to a great extent credited to crafted by Muhammad Yunus and the Grameen Bank in Bangladesh. Microfinance foundations (MFIs) are fundamental to the arrangement of these monetary administrations, working in both provincial and metropolitan settings, taking care of clients needing little, transient advances.

One of the essential targets of microfinance and credit programs is to reduce destitution. Admittance to monetary assets enables people to put resources into pay creating exercises, begin or extend independent ventures, and answer startling monetary difficulties. Thusly, these projects make pathways for financial independence and lessen reliance on magnanimous guide.

Notwithstanding destitution mitigation, microfinance and credit programs assume a vital part in advancing monetary consideration. A large number of individuals, especially in emerging nations, remain barred from the conventional financial area. Microfinance organizations give them the chance to save, acquire, and access other monetary administrations that are generally inaccessible. This incorporation can work on financial dependability and strength among the minimized and underserved populaces.

Enabling Ladies: One of the momentous results of microfinance programs is their capacity to engage ladies. In numerous social orders, ladies face monetary rejection, restricted admittance to assets, and limitations on financial support. Microfinance programs effectively target ladies as clients, empowering them to become business people, put resources into schooling and medical services for their families, and gain monetary autonomy. Research has shown that enabling ladies through microfinance decidedly affects family prosperity and local area advancement.

Work Creation: Little and miniature ventures are critical supporters of work in numerous economies. By offering monetary help to these ventures, microfinance and credit programs invigorate work creation. This occupation development benefits business visionaries as well as the more extensive local area by diminishing joblessness and further developing pay levels.

Versatility Even with Shocks: Microfinance and advance projects assist people and networks with building flexibility despite monetary shocks, like catastrophic events, wellbeing crises, or financial slumps. Approaching investment funds and credit can empower individuals to weather conditions emergencies and recuperate all the more rapidly, limiting the drawn out influence on their prosperity.

Improving Instruction and Medical care: Admittance to monetary assets can likewise straightforwardly affect admittance to training and medical care. Microfinance advances can be utilized to cover school expenses, buy instructive materials, or put resources into professional preparation.

Also, they can be used to pay for medical care costs, including clinic bills, drugs, and preventive administrations. These speculations not just further develop the prosperity of people and families yet in addition affect the improvement of human resources.

Social and Local area Improvement: Microfinance and advance projects frequently cultivate social and local area advancement by empowering aggregate activity and gathering based loaning models. Bunch loaning philosophies, for example, self improvement gatherings and local area based investment funds, make a feeling of responsibility and shared help among borrowers. These drives add to social attachment and local area advancement, as people cooperate to accomplish normal monetary objectives.

Monetary Incorporation and Monetary Development: The advancement of monetary consideration through microfinance has more extensive financial ramifications. By stretching out admittance to monetary administrations to a bigger portion of the populace, nations can invigorate financial development and lessen pay disparity. As individuals get sufficiently close to capital and monetary assets, they can partake all the more effectively in financial exercises, encouraging generally speaking monetary turn of events.

In spite of the various advantages related with microfinance and credit programs, there are likewise difficulties and worries that should be tended to.

Loan fees and Obligation: One of the main reactions of microfinance is the exorbitant financing costs charged by some microfinance establishments. While MFIs frequently legitimize these rates by refering to the higher regulatory expenses related with serving low-pay clients, finding some kind of harmony between monetary manageability and the gamble of over-obligation among borrowers is pivotal. Over-obligation can prompt a pattern of obligation and monetary trouble, subverting the expected destitution mitigation objectives.

Functional Maintainability: Microfinance establishments, especially those serving remote and underserved regions, face functional difficulties, for example, restricted framework, high exchange costs, and the requirement for talented faculty. Guaranteeing the supportability and adequacy of these establishments requires tending to these functional limitations.

Guideline and Buyer Insurance: The guideline of microfinance is fundamental to shield borrowers from ruthless loaning rehearses and guarantee fair treatment. Guideline ought to figure out some kind of harmony between cultivating a strong climate for MFIs and shielding borrowers. Finding some kind of harmony can be testing and fluctuates from one country to another.

Absence of Expansion: Numerous microfinance establishments center basically around giving credit, with restricted broadening into reserve funds, protection, and other monetary administrations. Broadening their contributions can work on monetary consideration and flexibility among their clients.

Supportability and Effect: Surveying the drawn out maintainability and effect of microfinance and credit programs is complicated. While they can emphatically affect people and networks, they are not a one-size-fits-all arrangement. The drawn out effect of these projects on destitution decrease, monetary turn of events, and monetary incorporation requires cautious and continuous assessment.

Advancements in Microfinance: New advances and developments are reshaping the microfinance scene. Versatile banking, advanced installments, and shared loaning stages are extending the span and proficiency of microfinance administrations. These developments give valuable chances to defeat conventional difficulties and proposition more savvy answers for clients.

Strategy and Government Backing: Government backing and strategy structures can assume a urgent part in improving the viability of microfinance and credit programs. Policymakers ought to zero in on establishing an empowering climate that supports capable loaning rehearses, advances monetary education, and encourages development in monetary administrations.

Social Effect Effective financial planning: The ascent of social effect money management offers an elective way to deal with subsidizing microfinance drives. Influence financial backers look for both a monetary profit from their ventures and a quantifiable positive social and natural effect. This approach can draw in confidential funding to microfinance and advance projects, growing their range and effect.

Joint effort and Associations: Cooperation between microfinance foundations, state run administrations, non-legislative associations, and worldwide organizations can prompt more complete and viable arrangements. Cooperating, these partners can use their ability, assets, and organizations to address complex difficulties, like destitution decrease, monetary consideration, and social turn of events.

6.3 Community Support and Networking

Local area support and systems administration are fundamental parts of human culture that work with association, help, and the trading of assets among people and gatherings. These basic parts of public activity act as essential starting points for individual prosperity and aggregate strength. In this paper, we will investigate the meaning of local area support and systems administration, their effect on people and networks, and the difficulties and valuable open doors they present.

At the core of local area support and systems administration lies the idea of common help. Networks are contained people who share normal interests, objectives, or topographical areas. These people meet up to give close to home, down to earth, and social help to each other. Whether through proper associations or casual organizations, local area support fills in as a life saver during critical crossroads and enhances the regular routines of its individuals.

One of the essential advantages of local area support and systems administration is the feeling of having a place it encourages. People are innately friendly creatures, and a sensation of association with others is fundamental for generally prosperity. Having a place with a local area, whether it's an area, a strict gathering, an interest-based club, or a web-based discussion, gives a feeling of character and motivation, diminishing sensations of detachment and depression.

Besides, people group support is a wellspring of close to home prosperity. At the point when people face individual difficulties or emergencies, like disease, misfortune, or profound pain, the presence of a strong local area can give solace and comfort. The demonstration of imparting encounters and feelings to others can ease the weights of life and advance mental and close to home flexibility.

Local area support isn't restricted to close to home prosperity; it likewise significantly affects actual wellbeing. Various investigations have shown that individuals with solid social associations will generally live longer, have better actual wellbeing, and experience lower levels of pressure. Drawing in with a steady local area can support better ways of life, increment admittance to assets, and give a security net during seasons of disease or handicap.

Notwithstanding individual prosperity, local area support and systems administration add to the general turn of events and attachment of networks. They work with the trading of assets, information, and abilities among local area individuals. For example, local area based associations might give instructive projects, work preparing, and admittance to medical care administrations, improving the personal satisfaction for their individuals. The sharing of information and abilities assists with building a more educated and fit local area.

Local area backing can likewise drive social and social change. Local area associations frequently advocate for purposes, put together occasions, and take part in exercises that address neighborhood and worldwide issues. Grassroots developments and local area drove drives are fundamental drivers of social advancement, pushing for changes in approaches, standards, and practices that can further develop the prosperity of society in general.

Organizing inside networks expands the range of help and assets. It permits local area individuals to take advantage of the aggregate aptitude and associations of the gathering. For instance, in an expert setting, systems administration can prompt open positions, professional success, and expertise improvement. In an individual setting, it can give admittance to childcare administrations, help with home fixes, or direction on exploring medical services frameworks.

Organizing inside networks likewise assumes a basic part in monetary turn of events. Organizations and business people frequently depend on nearby organizations to get to likely clients, financial backers, and teammates. These organizations set out monetary open doors and add to the monetary prosperity of the two people and the local area overall.

Besides, the cooperative idea of local area support and systems administration upgrades local area flexibility. Despite emergencies, whether they are cataclysmic events, monetary downturns, or general wellbeing crises, networks areas of strength for with networks are better prepared to answer and recuperate. They can prepare assets, share data, and direction endeavors to alleviate the effect of these difficulties.

While people group support and systems administration offer various advantages, they are not without difficulties and limits. These difficulties frequently emerge from variables like the size of the local area, the variety of its individuals, and changes in cultural elements.

One normal test is the adaptability of local area support. More modest, very close networks frequently have deeply grounded encouraging groups of people, however bigger and more different networks might battle to cultivate areas of strength for an of having a place and shared help. Keeping a feeling of local area for a bigger scope can be testing, particularly in metropolitan regions where people might have restricted communications with their neighbors.

Variety inside networks can likewise introduce difficulties. Comprehensive and fair encouraging groups of people ought to guarantee that all local area individuals feel appreciated and esteemed. Guaranteeing that minimized gatherings inside a local area approach similar degree of help and valuable open doors as others is fundamental for cultivating a feeling of incorporation and union.

Additionally, changing cultural elements, remembering the ascent of innovation and movements for work designs, can affect local area support and systems administration. While innovation can interface people across geological distances, it can likewise prompt a diminishing in eye to eye communications and an ascent in web-based networks, which may not give a similar degree of profound and viable help.

The speedy, current way of life can likewise present difficulties to local area support. Many individuals are overpowered with work and family responsibilities, allowing for dynamic cooperation in local area exercises and encouraging groups of people. This can bring about a decrease in local area union and a feeling of separation from others.

The advancement of local area support and systems administration requires proactive endeavors from the two people and networks, as well as cultural and strategy level changes.

At the singular level, dynamic cooperation and commitment to one's local area are fundamental. This might include chipping in, joining local area associations, or basically connecting with neighbors and colleagues. Being a functioning individual from the local area and offering backing to others can assist with cultivating a more grounded feeling of having a place and common help.

Local area pioneers and associations likewise assume a fundamental part in advancing local area support and systems administration. They can set out stages and open doors for local area individuals to associate, share, and team up. Such drives might incorporate area watch programs, local area gardens, ability sharing occasions, or social celebrations that praise the variety of the local area.

Cultural changes ought to perceive the significance of local area support and systems administration. Strategies that help local area building drives, dispense assets for local area improvement, and encourage a feeling of consideration are significant. These arrangements can go from metropolitan arranging that urges local area spaces to instructive projects that show the worth of local area commitment.

Innovation can be bridled to fortify local area support and systems administration. Online stages and virtual entertainment can work with associations and correspondence inside networks. In any case, it is essential to adjust the advantages of computerized network with the requirement for up close and personal communications, which cultivate a more profound feeling of local area.

Chapter 7

Sustainability and Environmental Responsibility

Maintainability and natural obligation have become principal ideas in the cutting edge world. As the human populace proceeds to develop, and our exercises apply expanding tension on the indigenous habitat, we genuinely must take on an all encompassing way to deal with guarantee the prosperity of both current and people in the future. This paper dives into the perplexing connection among maintainability and ecological obligation, investigating their importance, difficulties, and expected arrangements.

At its center, manageability incorporates the thought of addressing the necessities of the present without compromising the capacity of people in the future to address their own issues. This idea, frequently connected with the 1987 Brundtland Report, underlines the significance of adjusting financial, social, and natural parts of human life. The relationship of these elements is vital, as dismissing one can sabotage the maintainability of the others. Thus, advancing manageability implies considering the drawn out results of our activities and looking for harmony in our quest for progress.

Ecological obligation, then again, suggests recognizing our effect on the normal world and making moves to limit hurt and safeguard the climate. This obligation reaches out to people, associations, states, and the worldwide local area. It involves rehearses that decrease contamination, limit asset consumption, moderate biodiversity, and alleviate the impacts of environmental change. Generally, natural obligation expects us to be stewards of the planet, perceiving that our activities have expansive repercussions on the wellbeing and soundness of biological systems.

The earnestness of tending to supportability and ecological obligation couldn't possibly be more significant. Our planet is confronting various ecological difficulties that compromise the actual underpinning of life as far as we might be concerned. Environmental change, biodiversity misfortune, deforestation, natural surroundings obliteration, contamination, and asset shortage are among the major problems that request prompt consideration. The outcomes of inaction are now obvious, as outrageous climate occasions, rising ocean levels, and the deficiency of basic environments upset social orders and risk endless species.

One of the essential elements driving these natural difficulties is the manner in which we create and consume energy. Petroleum derivatives, which have long filled in as the foundation of the worldwide energy framework, discharge ozone depleting substances while copied, adding to the nursery impact and an unnatural weather change.

Progressing to manageable, low-carbon energy sources is a critical stage in relieving environmental change and lessening our ecological effect. Environmentally friendly power innovations, for example, sunlight based, wind, and hydropower, offer a way toward a more practical energy future. Outfitting these sources, in any case, requires significant venture, mechanical development, and a change in cultural standards.

The progress to supportable energy is only one feature of a more extensive change expected for worldwide manageability. Accomplishing ecological obligation requires a significant reevaluating of our utilization examples and creation processes. The direct "take-make-squander" model of asset use should be supplanted with round frameworks that focus on reusing, reusing, and lessening waste. This shift can prompt more effective asset use, lower energy utilization, and decreased ecological debasement.

Besides, the idea of supportability reaches out to financial frameworks. Generally, monetary development has been likened with progress, frequently estimated by GDP (Gross domestic product). In any case, this approach doesn't represent natural and social expenses. The quest for boundless development on a limited planet is impractical. Progressing to a maintainable economy requires a reconsideration of our monetary markers, perceiving the worth of normal capital and human prosperity. The improvement of elective pointers, like the Certified Advancement Marker (GPI), can assist with directing strategy and decision-production toward a more economical future.

One more key part of manageability and ecological obligation is the protection of biodiversity. The deficiency of biodiversity not just diminishes the planet's versatility to ecological changes yet in addition compromises the multifaceted trap of life that upholds human life. Endeavors to secure and reestablish biodiversity incorporate living space protection, species preservation, and reasonable land use rehearses. In addition, the significance of biological systems as carbon sinks, water purifiers, and food sources features the need of protecting their wellbeing.

Maintainability and ecological obligation are complicatedly connected with civil rights. It is fundamental to perceive that natural difficulties lopsidedly influence weak populaces, frequently intensifying existing disparities. Environmental change, for example, can prompt food and water shortage, uprooting, and struggle, with underestimated networks enduring the worst part of the results. Addressing these incongruities requires an impartial way to deal with supportability, one that guarantees admittance to assets, valuable open doors, and advantages for all.

The significance of reasonable improvement is revered in peaceful accords, including the Unified Countries Maintainable Advancement Objectives (SDGs). The SDGs frame a far reaching system for tending to many worldwide difficulties, from destitution and craving to clean energy and environment activity. Accomplishing these objectives requires participation at nearby, public, and worldwide levels, as well as the commitment of states, organizations, common society, and people.

Regardless of the unmistakable goals and worldwide responsibilities, manageability and natural obligation face various difficulties. Beating these impediments is a perplexing and diverse undertaking. One of the basic difficulties is the momentary center that frequently rules dynamic in both general society and confidential areas. Political cycles, quarterly monetary reports, and prompt satisfaction can impede long haul arranging and interest in maintainable practices.

One more test is the protection from change. Many laid out enterprises, especially those dependent on petroleum derivatives, have a personal stake in keeping up with the norm. Progressing to additional feasible practices can upset existing power designs and lead to financial disengagement. Thusly, the idleness of customary frameworks can be a critical hindrance to advance.

What's more, the absence of mindfulness and schooling about maintainability issues can block significant activity. Many individuals may not completely handle the results of their activities on the climate or comprehend how little changes in conduct can add to more extensive maintainability objectives. Successful correspondence and schooling are vital for address this hole and engage people to go with informed decisions.

Asset shortage and overexploitation present further difficulties. As the worldwide populace keeps on developing, the interest for assets like freshwater, arable land, and minerals increments. Unreasonable extraction and utilization practices can drain these assets, prompting clashes and ecological debasement. Tracking down ways of addressing the requirements of a developing populace while shielding the climate is a considerable undertaking.

Political and administrative hindrances can likewise prevent manageability endeavors. At times, state run administrations might come up short on will or ability to implement natural guidelines. In addition, political struggles and international interests can hinder global collaboration on ecological issues, as found in banters over environment arrangements and biodiversity security.

The expenses related with reasonable innovations and practices can be a huge impediment. While the drawn out advantages of manageability are clear, the underlying speculations required can be overwhelming, especially for people and private ventures. Admittance to capital, motivations, and steady approaches are essential for making supportability more open and reasonable.

Regardless of these difficulties, there are various arrangements and methodologies to advance maintainability and ecological obligation. Coordinated effort between legislatures, organizations, and common society is fundamental to create and execute strategies that help reasonable practices. Legislatures can give motivations, appropriations, and tax cuts to empower the reception of clean energy innovations and supportable farming. They can likewise set aggressive natural targets and authorize guidelines to restrict contamination and safeguard biological systems.

Organizations assume a critical part in driving maintainability. Corporate obligation drives, reasonable store network the executives, and the mix of ecological contemplations into business methodologies can assist with lessening the natural effect of the confidential area. Besides, organizations that focus on supportability frequently track down it helpful with regards to notoriety, client dependability, and long haul benefit.

People likewise play a basic part to play in the maintainability condition. Little way of life changes, like lessening energy utilization, limiting waste, and supporting reasonable items, can all things considered have a huge effect. Also, deciding in favor of naturally cognizant strategies and supporting associations that advance supportability can impact the more extensive direction of ecological obligation.

7.1 Eco-Friendly Practices in Small-Scale Industries

Limited scope businesses, frequently alluded to as little and medium-sized undertakings (SMEs), assume a significant part in monetary turn of events, creating work, encouraging business, and adding to neighborhood economies. Nonetheless, they are not excluded from the ecological difficulties and obligations that bigger businesses face. Lately, there has been a developing acknowledgment of the requirement for limited scope enterprises to embrace eco-accommodating practices. This paper investigates the importance, difficulties, and expected answers for executing maintainable and eco-accommodating practices in limited scope enterprises.

The Meaning of Eco-Accommodating Practices in Limited scope Enterprises

Limited scope enterprises are different in nature, enveloping a large number of exercises, from assembling and horticulture to administrations and retail. While they may not separately match the size of enormous enterprises, their combined effect on the climate can be significant. In numerous nations, SMEs are a prevailing monetary power, making it basic to address their natural impression.

Eco-accommodating practices in limited scope ventures are huge because of multiple factors. Most importantly, they add to diminishing the natural effect of modern exercises. By embracing rehearses that advance asset proficiency, lessen waste, and breaking point contamination, limited scope ventures can have an impact in moderating environmental change, saving regular assets, and safeguarding biological systems.

Additionally, eco-accommodating practices can improve the intensity of limited scope enterprises. Customers, financial backers, and administrative bodies progressively favor organizations that exhibit a guarantee to maintainability. Eco-accommodating items and administrations can draw in a developing business sector fragment that values earth capable decisions. Furthermore, embracing green practices can prompt expense investment funds, as energy-effective activities and waste decrease measures can bring down creation costs.

Manageability in limited scope enterprises additionally cultivates versatility. By limiting their dependence on limited assets and diminishing their openness to cost vacillations, SMEs can all the more likely climate monetary vulnerabilities. For example, taking on sustainable power sources can make limited scope ventures less helpless against energy cost spikes.

Moreover, eco-accommodating practices can prompt development and expanded admittance to funding. Limited scope enterprises that put resources into innovative work to make more practical items and cycles can acquire an upper hand. These developments can draw in speculation from financial speculators and effect financial backers hoping to help maintainable organizations.

Challenges in Carrying out Eco-Accommodating Practices

Carrying out eco-accommodating practices in limited scope businesses isn't without its difficulties. These ventures frequently face asset requirements, restricted specialized aptitude, and administrative obstacles that can make taking on manageable practices troublesome.

Restricted Assets: Limited scope businesses normally have restricted monetary and HR. Putting resources into sustainable power frameworks, energy-effective hardware, or waste administration foundation can be expensive. Numerous SMEs battle to apportion the fundamental assets to execute eco-accommodating practices.

Absence of Specialized Information: Limited scope entrepreneurs might miss the mark on specialized information or skill expected to distinguish and carry out eco-accommodating practices. This information hole can keep them from settling on informed conclusions about asset proficient innovations or feasible creation strategies.

Administrative Consistence: Limited scope ventures might find it trying to explore and conform to ecological guidelines. These guidelines can differ by district and industry, adding intricacy to the consistence cycle. More modest ventures may likewise miss the mark on legitimate and administrative ability to guarantee they fulfill natural guidelines.

Protection from Change: A few limited scope ventures might be impervious to change, especially in the event that they have worked in customary ways for a long time. Changing to eco-accommodating practices might require a social shift inside the association and beating opposition from representatives and the board.

Admittance to Funding: Admittance to supporting for green drives can be a significant obstacle for SMEs. While bigger organizations might have more noteworthy admittance to capital business sectors and green venture reserves, more modest undertakings might battle to get credits or draw in financial backers for manageability projects.

Expected Answers for Eco-Accommodating Practices

To defeat these difficulties and advance eco-accommodating practices in limited scope businesses, different methodologies and arrangements can be executed:

Government Backing and Motivating forces: Legislatures can assume a basic part in empowering eco-accommodating practices among limited scope enterprises. They can give monetary motivators, like awards, endowments, and tax reductions, to assist SMEs with putting resources into reasonable innovations. Also, state run administrations can improve and smooth out ecological guidelines, making consistence more open for more modest organizations.

Admittance to Specialized Help: Giving specialized help and preparing to limited scope enterprises can assist with spanning the information hole. Government organizations, NGOs, and industry affiliations can offer direction on feasible practices and assist SMEs with recognizing financially savvy answers for decreasing their natural impression.

Joint effort and Systems administration: Limited scope ventures can profit from teaming up with industry affiliations, research establishments, and different organizations. Sharing information and best practices through systems administration can assist SMEs with taking on eco-accommodating practices all the more successfully. Cooperative endeavors can likewise prompt shared assets, lessening the monetary weight of supportability drives.

Green Accreditation Projects: Green confirmation projects can assist SMEs with promoting their eco-accommodating items and administrations. These projects frequently give outsider approval of a business' manageability endeavors, which can be a significant selling point for purchasers.

Admittance to Funding: Monetary foundations and financial backers can make explicit monetary items intended to help eco-accommodating drives in limited scope businesses. These items might incorporate green advances or effect ventures designated at organizations focused on ecological obligation.

Preparing and Instruction: Instructive establishments and professional instructional hubs can offer courses and studios that emphasis on supportability and eco-accommodating practices. These projects can outfit representatives and business people with the information and abilities expected to execute green drives.

Innovation Sharing: Joint efforts and organizations with bigger organizations can furnish limited scope ventures with admittance to state of the art advancements and skill. These organizations can assist SMEs with taking on asset proficient and eco-accommodating advancements that could somehow or another be past their range.

Buyer Training and Request: Raising shopper mindfulness about the natural effect of items and administrations can drive interest for eco-accommodating choices. Shopper request can urge limited scope ventures to embrace maintainable practices to meet market inclinations.

Mentorship and Backing: Experienced maintainability experts and business people can act as coaches to limited scope industry proprietors and supervisors. Their direction and backing can assist SMEs with exploring the intricacies of maintainability and settle on informed decisions.

Eco-accommodating practices in limited scope enterprises are not just attractive for lessening the natural effect of these organizations yet additionally fundamental for their drawn out seriousness and strength. While limited scope businesses face one of a kind difficulties in embracing manageable practices, a blend of government support, admittance to specialized information, cooperation, certificate, and monetary impetuses can prepare for significant change.

By tending to these difficulties and advancing manageable practices, limited scope businesses can add to the worldwide work to battle environmental change, preserve regular assets, and safeguard biological systems. Besides, embracing eco-accommodating practices can upgrade the standing of limited scope organizations, draw in eco-cognizant buyers, and drive development inside the area. Chasing eco-accommodating practices, limited scope ventures can turn out to be naturally mindful as well as financially supportable and prosperous.

7.2 Reducing Carbon Footprints

The idea of diminishing carbon impressions has acquired expanding unmistakable quality as the world wrestles with the difficulties of environmental change and natural debasement. A carbon impression alludes to the aggregate sum of ozone harming substances, essentially carbon dioxide (CO_2), created straightforwardly and by implication by an individual, association, occasion, or item over its life cycle. These outflows, essentially coming about because of the consuming of petroleum products for energy and transportation, add to an unnatural weather change and other natural issues. This paper dives into the meaning of decreasing carbon impressions, the difficulties in question, and the different procedures and arrangements accessible to moderate this basic issue.

The Meaning of Diminishing Carbon Impressions

Diminishing carbon impressions is critical for a few convincing reasons. It is characteristically attached to the all-encompassing objective of relieving environmental change and its expansive results. Environmental change, driven by the gathering of ozone harming substances in the climate, prompts climbing worldwide temperatures, more regular and serious outrageous climate occasions, ocean level ascent, and disturbances to biological systems. It represents a grave danger to human social orders, natural life, and the general wellbeing of the planet.

Besides, carbon impressions are firmly connected to energy utilization, with a critical piece of ozone depleting substance emanations beginning from the energy area. A central change to low-carbon and environmentally friendly power sources is fundamental for lessening fossil fuel byproducts and limiting dependence on petroleum products. This progress mitigates environmental change as well as adds to energy security and supportability.

The decrease of carbon impressions is likewise fundamental for air quality and general wellbeing. The consuming of petroleum derivatives in vehicles and power plants discharges CO2 as well as contaminations that can hurt human wellbeing.

Brown haze, particulate matter, and different toxins from these sources are related with respiratory sicknesses, cardiovascular issues, and unexpected losses. By changing to cleaner energy and transportation frameworks, social orders can decrease the emanations of these hurtful contaminations and further develop air quality.

Notwithstanding environmental change and general wellbeing, the protection of regular assets is a key thought. Petroleum derivative extraction and utilization exhaust limited saves, while the development of labor and products frequently prompts the extraction of non-sustainable assets and natural surroundings annihilation. Decreasing carbon impressions includes limiting asset use and advancing manageability, which can assist with saving environments, biodiversity, and the planet's ability to help life.

7.3 Supporting Local Sourcing

In an undeniably globalized world, where items and administrations can be obtained from anyplace in the world, the idea of supporting neighborhood obtaining has acquired huge significance. Nearby obtaining, frequently advocated by defenders of manageability, local area improvement, and financial flexibility, is tied in with leaning toward labor and products delivered inside one's own district or local area. While globalization has without a doubt brought various advantages, for example, admittance to a wide cluster of items and administrations at serious costs, it has likewise brought about a few unseen side-effects, including ecological debasement, the debilitating of nearby economies, and a deficiency of local area character. To address these difficulties, numerous people, organizations, and state run administrations are perceiving the benefit of supporting nearby obtaining.

One of the essential contentions for nearby obtaining is the potential for ecological advantages. At the point when items are obtained locally, the carbon impression related with transportation is altogether decreased. Delivering merchandise across the world, whether via ocean, air, or land, consumes significant energy and produces discharges that add to environmental change. By inclining toward nearby items and administrations, purchasers and organizations can assist with diminishing these emanations and advance a more feasible future. In addition, supporting nearby obtaining can prompt more economical agrarian practices, as neighborhood ranchers are many times more put resources into keeping up with the strength of their territory and environments, contrasted with enormous scope, far off corporate activities. This can prompt less pesticide and herbicide applications, more proficient water use, and better soil the board, which thus can help the climate.

Besides, nearby obtaining essentially affects neighborhood economies. At the point when buyers and organizations focus on items and administrations from inside their own local area, they add to the development and solidness of nearby organizations. Little and privately claimed endeavors are essential to the wellbeing of local economies, as they make occupations, invigorate financial development, and keep cash coursing inside the local area.

Conversely, worldwide obtaining frequently brings about the convergence of abundance in the possession of a couple of huge companies, which can prompt financial disparity and the disintegration of nearby organizations. Supporting neighborhood obtaining reinforces the nearby work market as well as helps construct a stronger economy, as networks become less reliant upon outside hotspots for their essential necessities.

Nearby obtaining likewise assumes a pivotal part in protecting the one of a kind person and character of a local area. At the point when networks depend on worldwide obtaining, they risk losing their peculiarity as their nearby customs and societies are eclipsed by a homogenized worldwide market. By embracing neighborhood items, shoppers can assist with supporting the remarkable flavors, artworks, and customs that make their local area exceptional. Neighborhood obtaining upholds craftsmans and skilled workers who make items that mirror the way of life and history of their district, guaranteeing that these customs are passed down to people in the future. This not just improves the social legacy of a local area yet in addition upgrades its allure as a traveler objective, driving extra income to the area.

Notwithstanding ecological, financial, and social advantages, nearby obtaining can likewise emphatically affect the quality and wellbeing of items. At the point when merchandise are delivered locally, it is frequently more straightforward to follow their beginnings and creation strategies, which can prompt more prominent straightforwardness and responsibility. Customers can have more trust in the security and nature of items that come from their own local area, as they might have direct admittance to the makers and can ask about creation techniques and fixing sources. This straightforwardness is particularly significant in the food business, where worries about food handling and realness are common. By supporting neighborhood obtaining, customers can have more command over the quality and security of the items they buy.

One test in advancing nearby obtaining is the apparent expense distinction. Nearby items and administrations are in some cases apparent as more costly than their worldwide partners. This discernment is established in a few variables, for example, economies of scale delighted in by bigger makers, lower work costs in a few worldwide districts, and the potential for admittance to less expensive unrefined components. In any case, the genuine expense of worldwide obtaining frequently incorporates stowed away externalities, like transportation emanations and the disintegration of neighborhood economies. At the point when these externalities are thought of, the cost contrast among neighborhood and worldwide items may not be basically as huge as it at first shows up. Besides, a few shoppers will pay a premium for neighborhood items, perceiving the more extensive advantages they bring to their local area and the climate.

Government strategies can assume a urgent part in supporting nearby obtaining. Policymakers can execute motivators and guidelines to urge organizations to locally source. These motivating forces might incorporate tax reductions, sponsorships, or special treatment in government acquirement. By establishing a positive climate for nearby organizations, legislatures can invigorate financial development inside their networks and advance supportability.

In addition, they can set quality and ecological guidelines that support neighborhood obtaining, guaranteeing that items meet specific rules for security and maintainability. Along these lines, state run administrations can assist with evening the odds and make nearby items more aggressive with their worldwide partners.

Coordinated effort among organizations and neighborhood networks is one more fundamental part of supporting nearby obtaining. Nearby organizations can effectively draw in with their networks, teaching purchasers about the advantages of neighborhood obtaining and assembling connections in light of trust and responsibility. Besides, organizations can cooperate to fortify the nearby store network, making networks that help each other's development. These coordinated efforts can prompt expanded proficiency, decreased costs, and improved item quality. Local area backing can be a strong driver for neighborhood organizations, as purchasers who feel associated with their local area are bound to incline toward nearby items and administrations.

The ascent of online business and computerized stages has likewise set out new open doors for nearby obtaining. Online commercial centers and conveyance administrations can interface neighborhood makers with a more extensive client base, permitting independent ventures to contact a more extensive crowd without the requirement for an actual retail facade. These computerized stages can assist neighborhood organizations with conquering a portion of the difficulties they face in rivaling bigger, worldwide ventures. They likewise offer buyers a helpful method for getting to nearby items and administrations, further advancing the neighborhood obtaining development.

Training and mindfulness are basic in advancing neighborhood obtaining. Numerous purchasers may not completely grasp the advantages of supporting neighborhood organizations and might be influenced by the accommodation of worldwide items. By bringing issues to light about the natural, financial, and social benefits of neighborhood obtaining, people can settle on additional educated decisions about the items they buy. Drives like "Purchase Neighborhood" crusades, local area occasions, and instructive projects can assist with spreading the message and urge customers to think about the effect of their decisions on their networks.

Chapter 8

Success Stories

Achievement is an all inclusive yearning, and the quest for it takes many structures across the different embroidery of human undertakings. Examples of overcoming adversity act as guides of motivation, offering verification that fantasies can be understood and deterrents survive. Whether in the fields of business, sports, amusement, science, or self-awareness, examples of overcoming adversity enthrall our minds and spur us to take a stab at our objectives. They encapsulate the human soul's steady assurance, strength, and inventiveness, displaying the capability of people and, at times, whole networks. This paper dives into an assortment of examples of overcoming adversity, investigating their normal topics, the illustrations they show us, and their getting through pertinence in our lives.

Business Examples of overcoming adversity

Business examples of overcoming adversity are perpetually well known, as they mirror the fantasies of many trying business visionaries. One such story is that of Jeff Bezos, who established Amazon in his carport in 1994. With a dream to make a web-based commercial center that sold books, Bezos perceived the capability of the web and the undiscovered interest for internet business. His constant quest for client driven greatness and advancement drove Amazon to turn into the worldwide goliath it is today. The vital focus point from Bezos' process is the significance of visionary initiative and a readiness to adjust to an impacting world.

Another famous example of overcoming adversity is that of Steve Occupations, who helped to establish Macintosh in his folks' carport in 1976. Occupations' persistent quest for greatness in plan and client experience prompted the making of historic items like the iPhone, iPad, and Mac. His story highlights the meaning of steady enthusiasm, development, and an unflinching spotlight on making items that really reverberate with buyers.

These accounts share normal subjects of visionary initiative, flexibility, development, and a steady obligation to greatness. They show that outcome in business frequently requires strength, a status to embrace change, and a profound comprehension of client needs. However, while business examples of overcoming adversity are frequently celebrated for their monetary accomplishments, achievement can take many structures, and the tales that move us go past the bounds of the corporate world.

Sports Examples of overcoming adversity

The universe of sports offers a mother lode of examples of overcoming adversity, each with its special mix of devotion, diligence, and ability. One of the most celebrated examples of overcoming adversity in late history is that of Serena Williams.

Ascending from an unassuming foundation, she vanquished the universe of tennis with sheer assurance and an enthusiasm for the game. Williams' story exhibits that progress in sports frequently requests persistent preparation, a serious soul, and the capacity to conquer misfortune.

Another enthralling games example of overcoming adversity is that of Michael Jordan, broadly viewed as one of the best b-ball players ever. Regardless of confronting starting misfortunes and questions, Jordan's tenacious drive to win drove him to six NBA titles and various honors. His process features the significance of difficult work, discipline, and a never-surrender disposition.

Sports examples of overcoming adversity underscore the job of discipline, strength, and the quest for greatness. They rouse us to stretch our physical and mental boundaries and advise us that achievement frequently follows predictable exertion and an energy for the game.

Amusement and Expressions Examples of overcoming adversity

The universe of amusement and human expressions overflows with people who have made a permanent imprint on the social scene. An excellent example of overcoming adversity is that of the Beatles, an English musical crew that re-imagined music during the 1960s. Their transient ascent from playing little clubs in Liverpool to becoming worldwide symbols represents the force of coordinated effort, imaginative virtuoso, and a readiness to try different things with new sounds.

One more rousing example of overcoming adversity in the diversion world is that of J.K. Rowling, the creator of the Harry Potter series. Rowling confronted various dismissals before her series turned into a worldwide peculiarity, selling more than 500 million duplicates. Her story delineates the significance of flexibility, self-conviction, and the capacity to persist through difficulty.

Diversion and expressions examples of overcoming adversity highlight the worth of innovative articulation, cooperation, and the mental fortitude to follow one's creative vision. They instruct us that the way to outcome in the realm of expressions is frequently set apart by hardships, however immovable faith in one's specialty can prompt groundbreaking accomplishments.

Science and Development Examples of overcoming adversity

Logical and mechanical progressions are driven by the energy and devotion of people who steer history. One such example of overcoming adversity is that of Marie Curie, the primary lady to win a Nobel Prize and the main individual to win Nobel

Prizes in two different logical fields: physical science and science. Her spearheading work on radioactivity reformed the area of science and lastingly affects the clinical and atomic ventures.

One more notable example of overcoming adversity in science is the Apollo 11 moon landing. In 1969, NASA effectively landed space travelers Neil Armstrong and Buzz Aldrin on the moon, denoting a noteworthy accomplishment in human investigation. This mission exemplified the force of joint effort, advancement, and the dauntlessness to try the impossible.

Science and development examples of overcoming adversity feature the significance of interest, devotion, and the quest for information. They advise us that earth shattering revelations frequently require long stretches of difficult work, the boldness to address existing standards, and the drive to investigate unfamiliar domains.

Self-awareness Examples of overcoming adversity

Examples of overcoming adversity in self-awareness and personal development move us to defeat life's difficulties and turned into our best selves. The tale of Oprah Winfrey is a brilliant illustration of individual change. From a turbulent youth set apart by difficulty and misuse, she rose to become quite possibly of the most persuasive medium magnates on the planet. Her process highlights the force of flexibility, mindfulness, and the capacity to transform misfortune into a wellspring of solidarity.

Another noteworthy example of overcoming adversity is that of Malala Yousafzai, a Pakistani extremist and Nobel laureate. Malala challenged the Taliban to advocate for young ladies' schooling, getting through a close lethal assault simultaneously. Her story shows the boldness to go to bat for what one has faith in, even despite grave risk.

Self-improvement examples of overcoming adversity feature the significance of mindfulness, flexibility, and the quest for a significant life. They advise us that the way to progress frequently includes defeating individual difficulties and involving them as venturing stones toward a more promising time to come.

Normal Topics in Examples of overcoming adversity

While examples of overcoming adversity length many fields and encounters, they share normal subjects that reverberate with individuals from varying backgrounds.

Strength: Achievement frequently includes confronting misfortune, difficulties, and difficulties. Strength, the capacity to return from hardships, is a common subject in examples of overcoming adversity. People who continue on through difficult stretches and keep up with their assurance will more often than not accomplish their objectives.

Vision: Effective people regularly have an unmistakable vision of what they need to accomplish. Whether it's beginning a business, succeeding in a game, or making a logical disclosure, having a distinct objective is an ongoing theme in these accounts.

Commitment: Achievement seldom works out by accident more or less. Devotion, the faithful obligation to try sincerely and remain fixed on one's objectives, is a critical fixing in numerous examples of overcoming adversity. Whether it's vast long periods of training, research, or imaginative work, commitment is the main impetus behind exceptional accomplishments.

Flexibility: In a quickly impacting world, versatility is a significant quality. Examples of overcoming adversity frequently include people who were able to embrace change, turn, and develop their systems to address new difficulties and open doors.

Energy: Enthusiasm for one's field or try is a common subject in examples of overcoming adversity. The energy and love for what one truly does frequently fuel the drive to succeed and have an effect.

8.1 Profiles of Local Businesses

Nearby organizations are the foundation of networks, adding to financial development, encouraging a feeling of character, and giving fundamental labor and products. Every nearby business has its novel story, from the enthusiastic proprietor's vision to the difficulties they face in a cutthroat commercial center. In this exposition, we investigate profiles of different nearby organizations, revealing insight into their accounts, commitments, and the examples they proposition to the two business people and buyers.

The Family-Claimed Bread shop: A Sample of Custom

Envision the fragrance of newly heated bread, the glow of a comfortable inside, and the recognizable essences of the nearby pastry shop. Such a spot epitomizes the quintessence of local area and custom, and it's not unexpected a family-possessed business that keeps this custom alive. These nearby pastry shops are something beyond spots to purchase bread and cakes; they are woven into the texture of their areas.

One such pastry kitchen is "Bread cook's Enjoyment," a family-possessed foundation that has been serving its local area for more than thirty years. The bread shop was begun by Sarah and John, a couple enthusiastic about baking. Their fantasy was to make an inviting space where individuals could relish scrumptious, newly prepared merchandise while feeling like piece of a bigger family. Throughout the long term, Pastry specialist's Enjoyment has developed into a darling foundation, known for its high quality bread, delicious cakes, and a warm, cordial air.

The progress of Bread cook's Enjoyment goes past the nature of its items. It's established in the family's obligation to making a real association with their clients. They get some margin to realize their regulars by name, recall their #1 treats, and give a feeling of having a place that bigger fastens frequently battle to reproduce. This individual touch keeps clients returning as well as encourages a profound feeling of local area inside the pastry shop.

Nonetheless, running a neighborhood pastry shop isn't without its difficulties. The ascent of huge box supermarkets and the comfort of web based shopping have represented a danger to little, family-possessed organizations. To counter this, Pastry specialist's Joy has adjusted by growing its web-based presence and offering home conveyance administrations, while as yet keeping up with its in-store engage. They figure out the significance of mixing custom with current comfort.

The example from Pastry specialist's Pleasure is clear: neighborhood organizations can flourish by zeroing in on client connections, saving practice, and adjusting to the evolving commercial center.

The Eco-Accommodating Store: A Pledge to Supportability

Manageability is a developing worry in this day and age, and customers are progressively looking for organizations that share their obligation to the climate. This shift has led to eco-accommodating shops, which offer manageable items and cultivate an earth cognizant local area.

"Green Shelter" is one such shop, claimed by Lisa, a business person intensely for economical living. This neighborhood business has some expertise in morally obtained and eco-accommodating items, from attire made of natural materials to reusable family things. The shop's name, Green Shelter, mirrors the proprietor's yearning to make a sanctuary for those hoping to diminish their natural impression.

What separates Green Safe house is its commitment to giving data and schooling to clients. Lisa and her group trust in making maintainability open, whether through item marks that obviously make sense of their natural advantages or customary studios on practical living. This proactive methodology not just enables clients to pursue eco-accommodating decisions yet in addition cultivates a local area of similar people who share a promise to the climate.

For Lisa, maintaining a business that lines up with her qualities is a wellspring of pride and satisfaction. Nonetheless, it's not without its difficulties. Practical items can here and there be more costly to source and make, which can prompt greater cost focuses. Lisa has tended to this test by instructing her clients about the drawn out cost reserve funds and ecological advantages of the items she offers.

Green Shelter's prosperity shows the way that a nearby business can have a significant effect by focusing on maintainability and effectively captivating with its local area to bring issues to light and advance eco-cognizant decisions. It additionally features the significance of offsetting values with reasonableness in business tasks.

The People group Book shop: A Center point of Information and Culture

Neighborhood book shops have for some time been adored as spots of scholarly investigation, local area meeting, and social enhancement.

They are spaces where individuals come to find new universes through writing, participate in significant discussions, and praise the composed word. In the time of computerized perusing, these foundations stay a loved piece of numerous networks.

One such neighborhood book shop is "Pages of Marvel," claimed by Imprint and Emily, a couple who are energetic about the force of books. Their store is in excess of a spot to purchase understanding material; it's a safe house for book darlings. From the second you stroll in, the comfortable climate, racks fixed with different titles, and the proprietors' warm welcome clarify that this is a spot committed to the delight of perusing.

Pages of Miracle likewise assumes a fundamental part in encouraging an affection for writing among the more youthful age. They have book clubs, perusing occasions for youngsters, and in any event, composing studios. The book shop has turned into a center for scholarly and social trade, with standard writer readings, book dispatches, and conversations on significant points.

Despite internet business monsters and advanced perusing, Pages of Miracle faces moves natural to numerous nearby book shops. Nonetheless, their accentuation on the individual touch, local area commitment, and advancing the extraordinary characteristics of actual books has empowered them to stay a darling establishment in their town. Clients who esteem the feeling of disclosure and the material experience of perusing keep on supporting the store.

The example from Pages of Miracle is that nearby book shops can flourish by offering something other than books; they can be a wellspring of social improvement, a spot for significant local area cooperation, and a conductor for encouraging an affection for perusing among individuals, all things considered.

The Local Burger joint: A Culinary Practice

Nearby coffee shops hold a unique spot in the hearts of networks. They are the go-to spots for solace food, a generous breakfast, or a late-night nibble. These foundations give something other than food; they are an impression of an area's culinary custom and a center point for neighborhood food lovers.

"Tony's Coffee shop" is one such neighborhood culinary diamond, claimed by Tony, an enthusiastic gourmet specialist and a mainstay of the local area. His cafe is known for its exemplary American passage, from delicious burgers to natively constructed pies. The warm and inviting air at Tony's Coffee shop is an encouragement to relish delectable food as well as the kinship of the regulars who accumulate at the counter or in the comfortable stalls.

What separates Tony's Burger joint is its obligation to utilizing new, privately obtained fixings. Tony's menu highlights dishes made with items from adjacent homesteads and providers, supporting neighborhood farming while at the same time conveying quality dinners to his clients. This approach not just improves the taste and nature of the food yet in addition adds to the supportability of the nearby economy.

Running a neighborhood coffee shop accompanies its special difficulties. Rising food costs, contest from inexpensive food chains, and changing purchaser inclinations require versatility and innovativeness. Tony's Burger joint tends to these difficulties by consistently refreshing the menu to reflect occasional fixings, offering everyday specials, and effectively captivating with the local area through occasions and pledge drives.

The progress of Tony's Cafe fills in as an update that neighborhood coffee shops can flourish by safeguarding culinary practices, utilizing privately obtained fixings, and making a feeling of local area inside their walls. These foundations offer something beyond food; they give a feeling of having a place and a sample of custom.

8.2 Resilience and Adaptation

Flexibility and variation are two major human characteristics that have been tried and sharpened over the entire course of time. They are qualities that enable people and networks to stand up to difficulty, defeat difficulties, and flourish despite change. Whether on an individual level or inside the more extensive setting of social orders, the capacity to return quickly from misfortunes and adjust to new conditions is fundamental for development, progress, and prosperity. In this article, we will dig into the ideas of flexibility and variation, investigating their importance, the elements that add to them, and the manners by which they are appeared in different parts of human existence.

Versatility: The Ability to Bounce back

Versatility is a complex idea that mirrors a person's or a local area's ability to endure and recuperate from testing circumstances, injury, or misfortune. It includes mental, profound, and social components that add to one's capacity to adapt to pressure, misfortune, and injury successfully. Strength is definitely not a proper characteristic but instead a powerful quality that can be created and improved after some time.

Individual strength frequently rises out of a mix of individual qualities, strong connections, and natural variables. Characteristics like idealism, confidence, flexibility, and a feeling of direction can reinforce a singular's versatility. Sustaining solid connections, looking for social help, and keeping a hearty encouraging group of people are likewise fundamental components of strength.

The job of early valuable encounters in forming a singular's flexibility can't be put into words. Unfavorable youth encounters, like maltreatment, disregard, or misfortune, can affect flexibility, yet they are not really deterministic. Numerous people who have encountered testing young lives can foster exceptional flexibility and proceed to lead satisfying lives. This represents the powerful idea of strength and the limit with regards to development and transformation.

Flexibility can appear in different ways in a singular's life. Notwithstanding misfortune, a versatile individual might show close to home strength, a critical thinking direction, and a readiness to look for help when required. They can explore stressors with effortlessness, quickly returning from mishaps, and in any event, involving difficulties as any open doors for self-improvement.

Variation: Flourishing in an Impacting World

Variation is a firmly related idea to flexibility, zeroing in on an individual or a local area's ability to conform to new conditions, challenges, or evolving conditions. While strength fundamentally addresses returning from misfortune, variation envelops the more extensive course of embracing change and flourishing in a unique world.

Mankind's set of experiences is loaded with instances of transformation in light of evolving conditions. From the advancement of farming to the development of the web, people have reliably adjusted to new conditions to work on their personal satisfaction. This versatile limit is a demonstration of the human capacity to learn, develop, and flourish in a steadily advancing world.

With regards to self-awareness, transformation implies the capacity to answer changing life conditions, make essential changes, and develop. Life is loaded with advances, including profession changes, migration, individual connections, and well-being challenges. Transformation expects people to be adaptable, open to learning, and able to change their objectives and plans depending on the situation.

The Crossing point of Flexibility and Variation

While versatility and variation are particular ideas, they are firmly interwoven. Strength can be seen as a primary component that empowers variation. At the point when people have the ability to return from affliction and keep up with their mental prosperity, they are bound to effectively explore change. Versatility gives the close to home and mental strength expected to move toward new difficulties with an uplifting perspective.

Then again, transformation sustains strength. At the point when people embrace change and show the capacity to flourish in new conditions, they support their healthy identity viability and their confidence in their capacity to beat difficulties. The fruitful route of progress can act as proof that an individual has the inner and outer assets important to fabricate flexibility.

Consider, for example, an individual who loses their employment startlingly. Their underlying reaction to this affliction might require strength — the capacity to adapt to the shock, profound pain, and vulnerability. In any case, their resulting activities will include transformation — like looking for new business amazing open doors, obtaining new abilities, and changing their monetary designs to oblige the change.

Versatility and Variation in Self-improvement

Versatility and variation assume a urgent part in self-improvement and advancement. They are the characteristics that permit people to confront life's inescapable difficulties, misfortunes, and advances and rise up out of them more grounded and more competent. Self-improvement is definitely not a direct cycle; it frequently includes standing up to and beating deterrents, which requires both versatility and transformation.

Consider the excursion of a youthful grown-up who ventures out from home interestingly to go to school. This progress is set apart by huge changes: new obligations, scholastic difficulties, and the need to lay out autonomy. The capacity to adjust to these progressions while keeping up with profound and mental prosperity requires versatility. The individual should figure out how to explore scholarly requests, assemble new informal communities, and deal with their time actually.

As the school experience unfurls, further transformations are required. Scholastic objectives might move, vocation goals might develop, and individual qualities and convictions might be refined. The course of transformation permits the person to make essential acclimations to line up with their developing comprehension of themselves and their position on the planet.

Over the course of life, self-improvement keeps on being set apart by times of progress, change, and change. Strength is essential for standing up to surprising affliction, while variation is the instrument through which people reconsider their objectives and foster new methodologies for contacting them. The cooperative energy between these two characteristics guarantees that self-awareness is a dynamic and deep rooted process.

Strength and Transformation in Connections

Flexibility and variation are not restricted to individual encounters; they are likewise essential with regards to relational connections. Connections, whether familial, heartfelt, or companionships, frequently experience difficulties and changes that require both strength and transformation to effectively explore.

In cozy connections, strength is the ability to endure the unavoidable contentions, conflicts, and difficulties that can emerge. Versatile people can oversee pressure and struggle valuably, convey really, and fix profound injuries. Versatility in connections permits people to keep up with their close to home bonds and feeling of association.

Variation in connections involves the capacity to change and become together. Individuals change over the long run, thus do their requirements and wants inside a relationship. Variation permits accomplices to oblige each other's developing inclinations, convey straightforwardly about their evolving assumptions, and track down better approaches to associate and support their relationship.

An exemplary illustration of the exchange among strength and transformation in connections can be tracked down with regards to a drawn out organization. Throughout the long term, couples frequently face huge difficulties, for example, profession changes, being a parent, or medical problems. The versatility of each accomplice is tried as they go up against these difficulties together. The capacity to impart, offer profound help, and find valuable arrangements is fundamental for keeping up with the strength of the relationship.

Transformation is similarly significant in this unique circumstance. As people in the organization develop and change, they should adjust to their new jobs and obligations. This could include rethinking their common objectives, obliging each other's developing necessities, and tracking down better approaches to keep a feeling of closeness and association.

Fruitful long haul connections frequently require continuous transformation to oblige the progressions that happen over the long haul. While flexibility assists accomplices with dealing with the unavoidable struggles and hardships, variation permits them to flourish in the changing scene of their relationship.

Versatility and Variation in Local area and Society

Strength and variation are not bound to individual encounters and relational connections; they likewise hold importance in the more extensive setting of networks and social orders. Networks should have the strength to endure outer shocks, like financial slumps, cataclysmic events, or general wellbeing emergencies.

Despite misfortune, strong networks are those that can retain the underlying effect of an emergency, rally together to offer help, and recuperate in a planned and coordinated way. They have the ability to adjust to new conditions, whether by changing their financial methodologies, upgrading foundation to relieve future dangers, or encouraging a culture of readiness.

8.3 Lessons from the Field

Life is a consistent excursion of learning, with each experience offering important examples. Nonetheless, probably the most significant and persevering through examples are frequently drawn from genuine encounters and the insight shared by the people who have wandered into different fields, going from business and schooling to human expression and sciences. In this paper, we investigate the important illustrations collected from the field, where people have pushed the limits of human information and accomplished exceptional accomplishments, filling in as guides of motivation and understanding for every one of us.

Business and Business: Illustrations in Development and Steadiness

The universe of business and business is loaded with significant examples, and one of the most resonating is the significance of advancement and steadiness. Effective business visionaries, like Elon Musk, have shown the extraordinary force of advancement in making weighty items and administrations.

Musk, the pioneer behind SpaceX and Tesla, has taken critical steps in space investigation and electric vehicles, testing regular reasoning and lighting an upheaval in the two enterprises.

One of the critical illustrations from Musk's process is the requirement for tireless development and the readiness to handle bold objectives. His endeavors are set apart by the quest for aggressive, long haul goals, from colonizing Mars to diminishing humankind's dependence on petroleum products. Musk's enduring obligation to development advises us that the most extraordinary forward leaps frequently require venturing into the obscure, facing challenges, and declining to acknowledge the state of affairs.

Determination is one more focal subject in the realm of business and business venture. The tale of Howard Schultz, the organizer behind Starbucks, embodies the significance of flexibility and assurance. Schultz confronted various difficulties in his quest for transforming Starbucks into a worldwide espresso force to be reckoned with. In any case, his unfaltering faith in the capability of the brand, combined with his flexibility notwithstanding misfortune, eventually prompted Starbucks' prosperity.

Examples from business and business venture highlight the meaning of development and the fortitude to seek after nervy objectives, in any event, when confronted with hindrances. The capacity to endure, adjust, and stay fearless even with difficulty is a sign of effective people in this field.

Instruction: Supporting a Long lasting Affection for Learning

In the domain of training, the important example of sustaining a long lasting adoration for learning sticks out. Teachers and thought pioneers like Sir Ken Robinson have supported the possibility that the schooling system ought to zero in on encouraging imagination, decisive reasoning, and a certified enthusiasm for learning.

Robinson's well known TED Talk, "Do Schools Kill Imagination?" moved the regular way to deal with training, featuring the significance of supporting individual abilities and encouraging inventiveness. He underscored the need to establish conditions where understudies are urged to investigate their novel advantages and foster an affection for learning.

One of the critical examples from the field of schooling is that learning is a long lasting excursion. It doesn't end with graduation; it ought to be a consistent course of investigation and revelation. Instructors and understudies the same ought to try to develop a profound interest on the planet and an energy for gaining information. This way to deal with learning enhances lives as well as gets ready people to adjust to an always impacting world.

Expressions and Imagination: Embracing Weakness and Credibility

The universe of expressions and innovativeness offers significant illustrations about weakness and legitimacy. Craftsmen like Brené Brown, an eminent specialist and narrator, have underscored the significance of weakness as a wellspring of innovativeness and association.

Earthy colored's work on disgrace, weakness, and sympathy significantly affects the manner in which individuals grasp the human experience.

One of the focal examples from the field of expressions and inventiveness is that embracing weakness is fundamental for making genuine and significant work. Being weak in one's innovative flow implies facing challenges, being available to analysis, and uncovering one's actual self through one's specialty. This legitimacy can prompt profoundly resounding and genuinely rich inventive articulations.

In a world frequently distracted with flawlessness and congruity, the example from human expressions is that realness, even with every one of its defects, is the wellspring of genuine imagination and association. It urges people to be proudly themselves and to communicate their one of a kind points of view and feelings through their work.

Science and Investigation: The Quest for Information and Disclosure

Science and investigation offer priceless illustrations chasing after information and disclosure. Pioneers like Jane Goodall, the prestigious primatologist and moderate, have shown the world the meaning of committed logical request and the protection of our regular world.

Goodall's work with chimpanzees in Gombe Stream Public Park changed how we might interpret primate conduct and the multifaceted connections inside biological systems. Her obligation to preservation and natural security has made her an image of the significance of protecting our planet.

One of the vital illustrations from the area of science and investigation is the enduring quest for information and the obligation to secure and safeguard the normal world. Goodall's work highlights that comprehension and safeguarding our planet isn't just a logical undertaking yet in addition an ethical objective.

Science and investigation move people to be interested about the world, to seek clarification on pressing issues, and to look for replies. They instruct us that information is a significant asset that can drive progress and work on the human condition.

Wellbeing and Health: The Force of Anticipation and Versatility

In the field of wellbeing and health, a huge illustration rotates around the force of counteraction and flexibility. Medical care experts and specialists like Dr. Anthony Fauci have highlighted the significance of proactive wellbeing measures and building versatility even with wellbeing challenges.

Fauci, the head of the Public Foundation of Sensitivity and Irresistible Sicknesses, assumed a basic part in directing the US through various wellbeing emergencies, including the HIV/Helps plague and the Coronavirus pandemic. His unfaltering obligation to science-based navigation and general wellbeing has made him a confided in figure in the field.

One of the vital examples from the field of wellbeing and health is the significance of proactive measures to forestall ailment and advance prosperity. Fauci's work shows the benefit of putting resources into research, general wellbeing framework, and logical mastery to address wellbeing challenges.

Strength is one more focal example from this field. Wellbeing and health specialists underscore the meaning of building flexibility in people and networks to endure wellbeing emergencies and adjust to evolving conditions. The capacity to return from misfortunes and keep up with mental and actual prosperity is a basic part of human wellbeing.

Examples from the Field: A Continuous Excursion of Revelation

The examples from different fields of human undertaking are not static; they are important for a continuous excursion of disclosure and development. They give important experiences into development, diligence, innovativeness, weakness, validness, information, and prosperity. These illustrations are not restricted to explicit spaces; they have all inclusive appropriateness and pertinence for all parts of life.

The vital important point from the examples of the field is that life is a ceaseless course of learning and development. Each experience, each test, and each pursuit offers a chance to acquire astuteness and enhance how we might interpret the world. The insight shared by people who have wandered into different fields fills in as a wellspring of motivation and understanding for every one of us.

These examples highlight the significance of development and the mental fortitude to face challenges, the need of sustaining a long lasting adoration for learning, the force of genuineness and weakness in imagination, the benefit of seeking after information and revelation, and the meaning of proactive wellbeing measures and strength notwithstanding challenges. They guide us on our own excursions of investigation and disclosure, empowering us to embrace the obscure, to advance consistently, and to genuinely live.

| 96 |

Chapter 9

Future Prospects and Conclusion

What's in store holds a bunch of conceivable outcomes and difficulties that will shape our reality in manners we can start to envision. From progresses in innovation to the developing scene of worldwide legislative issues, the next few years will be characterized by the crossing point of various patterns and powers. In this segment, we will investigate a portion of the key future possibilities that will probably influence our general public, economy, and climate.

Perhaps of the most huge and groundbreaking improvement not too far off is the proceeded with headway of man-made reasoning and mechanization. AI and computer based intelligence innovations are turning out to be progressively modern and are as of now reshaping businesses and the idea of work. While mechanization holds the commitment of expanded efficiency and effectiveness, it likewise raises worries about work relocation and the requirement for reskilling and upskilling the labor force.

In the field of medical services, what's to come guarantees energizing forward leaps in genomics and customized medication. Hereditary sequencing and altering advancements can possibly change the manner in which we treat illnesses and foster drugs. By fitting therapies to a person's hereditary cosmetics, we might possibly work on the adequacy of clinical mediations and lessen unfriendly secondary effects. In any case, moral and security concerns encompassing the utilization of hereditary information should be tended to as these advancements advance.

Environmental change is one more major problem that will keep on ruling the worldwide plan. The requirement for supportable energy sources and carbon decrease procedures is more basic than any time in recent memory. The progress to sustainable power, for example, sun based and wind power, offers a way to decreasing ozone depleting substance discharges, however it likewise requires huge speculation and strategy support. The future will be set apart by endeavors to moderate the impacts of environmental change and adjust to its ramifications.

In the domain of room investigation, what's to come holds guarantee with recharged revenue in lunar and Martian missions. Associations like NASA and privately owned businesses like SpaceX are dealing with plans to send people back to the Moon and ultimately to Mars. These aggressive undertakings could open up new boondocks for logical exploration, asset usage, and, surprisingly, the chance of human colonization of other heavenly bodies. Notwithstanding, the difficulties and dangers of room travel, including long-span missions and radiation openness, should be painstakingly tended to.

The computerized domain is likewise set for additional change. The development of the web of things (IoT) and the rising interconnectivity of gadgets will achieve a reality where regular items are connected to the web, empowering more noteworthy mechanization and information assortment. While this offers accommodation and productivity, it additionally raises worries about protection and security, as more private data becomes open through associated gadgets.

The fate of transportation is ready for significant changes too. Electric vehicles (EVs) are getting some decent momentum as state run administrations and customers the same perceive the need to decrease ozone depleting substance discharges from the transportation area. The advancement of independent vehicles, self-driving vehicles, and the extension of ride-sharing administrations are likewise set to reshape metropolitan versatility. These headways hold the possibility to further develop security, diminish gridlock, and alter the manner in which we ponder transportation, yet they likewise accompany administrative and moral difficulties.

The worldwide economy is probably going to encounter further moves and disturbances before very long. The continuous pattern of globalization will keep on molding exchange and supply chains, while exchange pressures and international struggles might affect worldwide financial dependability. Furthermore, the ascent of arising economies, especially in Asia, is ready to challenge the strength of conventional financial powers. As innovation and advancement keep on driving financial development, nations and businesses that adjust rapidly to these progressions will probably flourish from here on out.

The universe of schooling is likewise developing quickly. Web based learning and computerized stages have acquired unmistakable quality, offering more prominent admittance to schooling and preparing. The eventual fate of instruction will probably see a mix of conventional and computerized learning, customized educational plans, and an emphasis on abilities that are versatile to a quickly changing position market. Deep rooted learning will become fundamental for people to remain serious in the labor force.

In the domain of governmental issues and global relations, what's in store is set apart by the two difficulties and amazing open doors. Worldwide issues like psychological oppression, digital fighting, and the multiplication of atomic weapons will keep on requesting the consideration of policymakers. The ascent of populism and the disintegration of popularity based standards in certain regions of the planet present difficulties to worldwide administration and participation. Nonetheless, worldwide endeavors to resolve issues like environmental change and worldwide wellbeing emergencies show the potential for cooperation on a worldwide scale.

All in all, our reality is at a junction, balanced on the cusp of phenomenal change and change. The difficulties and potential open doors that lie ahead are monstrous, and the way in which we explore them will characterize the eventual fate of our general public, economy, and climate. It is a period of extraordinary commitment, as well as a period of incredible vulnerability.

The headways in innovation, especially in the fields of man-made consciousness, genomics, and space investigation, hold the possibility to change our lives in manners we can barely envision. These forward leaps offer answers for a portion of our most squeezing issues, from clinical medicines customized to our hereditary cosmetics to the chance of colonizing different planets as we endeavor to safeguard and protect our own.

The issue of environmental change poses a potential threat in our future, requesting prompt and supported activity. Our obligation to practical energy sources, carbon decrease, and environment variation will be basic in molding the world we leave for people in the future. We have the information and the instruments to address this test, however the clock is ticking.

The computerized age has achieved striking availability and comfort, yet it has additionally led to squeezing inquiries concerning protection, security, and the moral utilization of innovation. As we push ahead, we should figure out some kind of harmony between the advantages of an interconnected world and the potential dangers related with it.

The eventual fate of transportation is set to reshape the manner in which we move, offering the commitment of diminished emanations and expanded portability. However, the difficulties of controlling independent vehicles, guaranteeing wellbeing, and building the vital framework can't be undervalued.

Financially, we stand at a snapshot of change. As the worldwide economy keeps on advancing, it is occupant upon countries and businesses to adjust and improve. The ascent of arising economies presents new open doors for coordinated effort and rivalry, and the significance of a talented and versatile labor force couldn't possibly be more significant.

In the domain of training, we can possibly make learning more available and customized. The advanced age offers devices and stages that can enable people to acquire new abilities and information all through their lives, however it likewise expects us to resolve issues of access, quality, and correspondence in training.

The eventual fate of governmental issues and worldwide relations is set apart by the requirement for worldwide participation on issues going from environmental change to worldwide wellbeing security. We should explore complex international difficulties while maintaining vote based values and standards in our current reality where they are progressively under danger.

Despite these difficulties and amazing open doors, the job of people, networks, and countries is fundamental. Our decisions today will resound as the years progressed and shape the world we give to people in the future. It is a source of inspiration for us all to be educated, connected with, and proactive in resolving the major problems within recent memory.

As we plan ahead, we should likewise recollect the persevering through significance of values like sympathy, empathy, and collaboration. These qualities are the bedrock of a fair and impartial society, and they are fundamental in directing our activities and choices in a quickly impacting world.

9.1 The Role of Small-Scale Industries in Future Economies

Limited scope ventures, frequently alluded to as SMEs (Little and Medium-sized Undertakings), assume an imperative part in the monetary scene of countries across the world. As we look forward to the future, the meaning of limited scope businesses is probably going to develop significantly more articulated. These organizations, described by their size and degree, can possibly become significant drivers of monetary development, advancement, and occupation creation. In this conversation, we will investigate the basic job that limited scale ventures are ready to play in ongoing economies.

Limited scope enterprises are commonly characterized in view of models connected with the quantity of representatives, yearly income, or resources. Generally speaking, these organizations utilize less than a specific edge of representatives, frequently going from a couple to two or three hundred. Their yearly income and resources likewise will generally be on the more modest side contrasted with bigger companies. Be that as it may, these definitions can change starting with one country then onto the next.

One of the vital qualities of limited scope enterprises is their ability to produce work amazing open doors. As we move into the future, addressing joblessness and underemployment will keep on being really difficult for economies around the world. Limited scope ventures, with their ability to make occupations at the nearby level, can act as a urgent driver of business development. They frequently utilize people in a different scope of jobs, from creation and assembling to promoting, deals, and the board, adding to monetary steadiness and individual occupations.

Besides, limited scope businesses are much of the time more lithe and adaptable than their bigger partners. This flexibility can be a critical benefit in the quick moving and quickly changing scene representing things to come. More modest organizations can turn rapidly in light of market shifts, client inclinations, and arising advancements. They can explore different avenues regarding groundbreaking thoughts, enhance, and adjust, improving them fit to explore the vulnerabilities and disturbances that are normal before very long.

Advancement is another region where limited scope ventures can succeed. Later on, innovative headways will keep on forming enterprises and markets. Independent ventures, unrestricted by the organization and unbending designs of bigger companies, can cultivate a culture of development and trial and error. They frequently act as hatcheries for clever thoughts and approaches, which can therefore upset and change ventures. As we move into a period set apart by man-made brainpower, robotization, and the Web of Things, limited scope businesses might be at the bleeding edge of driving mechanical change.

Besides, limited scope enterprises are much of the time well established in their neighborhood networks. This association with neighborhoods lead to a scope of positive results. Neighborhood organizations will generally uphold the advancement of networks, through work creation as well as through the flow of capital inside the area. They frequently source their bits of feedbacks locally, which can help the interest for nearby items and administrations. This relationship can assist with making powerful and versatile nearby economies that are more ready to endure worldwide financial shocks.

Supportability is a vital thought for future economies, given the squeezing worries about environmental change and ecological corruption. Limited scope ventures, because of their size and restricted nature, are strategically situated to take on additional economical practices. They can frequently execute harmless to the ecosystem advancements and cycles no sweat and lower costs contrasted with enormous enterprises. Furthermore, their associations with nearby networks can cultivate a feeling of obligation towards the climate, empowering manageable practices and diminishing their carbon impression.

The ascent of web based business and advanced stages has additionally extended the span and open doors for limited scope enterprises. With the development of online commercial centers, private companies can get to a worldwide client base and rival bigger ventures on a more level battleground. This computerized change is supposed to keep, offering limited scope enterprises the opportunity to scale their tasks and contact a more extensive crowd.

Legislatures and policymakers play a critical part to play in supporting the development and improvement of limited scope ventures. Admittance to funding, instruction, and preparing are critical elements that can decide the progress of these organizations. Later on, state run administrations ought to zero in on establishing an empowering climate that upholds business, works with admittance to capital, and gives motivations to advancement and manageability. This help can come as awards, charge motivating forces, low-interest credits, and drives that empower coordinated effort between independent companies and exploration organizations.

Moreover, advancing the internationalization of limited scope ventures can open up new roads for development. Empowering commodities and encouraging associations with abroad business sectors can assist these organizations with taking advantage of worldwide open doors. States can likewise attempt to diminish exchange obstructions and work on product and import strategies, making it simpler for private companies to participate in global exchange.

The eventual fate of limited scope businesses isn't without challenges. These organizations frequently face limitations connected with admittance to capital, restricted assets for innovative work, and rivalry from bigger endeavors. Besides, they might come up short on economies of scale that bigger partnerships appreciate. These difficulties can be tended to through essential help from legislatures, coordinated effort with research establishments, and the development of industry groups to pool assets and information.

One more basic part representing things to come for limited scope ventures is digitalization. The reception of computerized advances and the coordination of information driven approaches can fundamentally improve their seriousness. This computerized change can empower these organizations to more readily grasp their clients, streamline their stockpile chains, and work on their items and administrations.

Worldwide stockpile chains are turning out to be progressively perplexing, with different parts of items being produced in various nations and afterward collected somewhere else. Limited scope ventures can track down open doors in this intricacy. They can become providers of particular parts or proposition specialty administrations inside these inventory chains. To do as such, they might have to put resources into cutting edge producing advances and foster aptitude in unambiguous regions.

As the total populace keeps on developing, food security and manageable horticulture will stay fundamental worries. Limited scope rural organizations, from family homesteads to neighborhood food makers, play a basic part to play in guaranteeing that individuals approach protected and nutritious food. The future will probably see an emphasis on working on horticultural works on, diminishing waste, and upgrading the manageability of food creation. Limited scope rural organizations can lead the way in these endeavors.

9.2 Key Takeaways and Reflections

As we venture through the different and dynamic points examined in this text, a scope of key action items and reflections arise. From investigating the profundities of computerized reasoning and the vast conceivable outcomes of room investigation to digging into the intricacies of environmental change and the job of limited scope enterprises, there are a few general subjects and experiences that merit our consideration. In this segment, we will distil the fundamental focuses and give a space to reflection on the aggregate information and thoughts introduced.

One focal topic that rises out of this conversation is the relentless walk of innovation. Computerized reasoning and robotization are reshaping businesses and the idea of work. What's in store guarantees significantly more complex computer based intelligence frameworks and mechanization, which, while upgrading efficiency, will likewise bring up issues about work removal and the requirement for persistent labor force preparing. The critical important point here is that we should embrace innovation while at the same time getting ready for the difficulties it presents. This requires a guarantee to long lasting learning and versatility.

Genomics and customized medication address a future where medical services is custom-made to a person's hereditary cosmetics. This offers the commitment of additional successful medicines and decreased incidental effects, yet it likewise delivers moral and protection concerns. The important point is that clinical progressions are a two sided deal, and we should explore these waters cautiously, with vigorous guidelines and a solid spotlight on understanding security and assent.

Environmental change is a characterizing challenge within recent memory, with a developing agreement on the requirement for reasonable energy sources and carbon decrease. The progress to environmentally friendly power, while offering expect moderating the impacts of environmental change, requires critical speculation and strategy support. The focus point is that tending to environmental change requires a worldwide, aggregate exertion. It isn't exclusively the obligation of states; people, networks, and enterprises all play parts to play in decreasing their carbon impression and upholding for maintainable practices.

Space investigation is near the precarious edge of invigorating new skylines, with plans to return people to the Moon and at last send them to Mars. These missions hold the commitment of logical disclosure and the chance of human colonization of other heavenly bodies. Nonetheless, they additionally bring impressive difficulties, from the physical and mental cost of long-term space travel to the moral contemplations of room colonization. The action item is that space investigation addresses the human soul's natural craving to investigate and grow. As we adventure into the universe, we should do as such with a solid obligation to research, security, and moral standards.

The advanced domain keeps on developing, with the web of things (IoT) associating regular items to the web. While this interconnectedness offers accommodation and productivity, it additionally raises worries about protection and security. The focus point is that the computerized age has conceded us phenomenal network and comfort yet has likewise put a top notch on protecting our own data and guaranteeing the security of advanced frameworks. As people, we should be watchful and educated clients regarding innovation.

The fate of transportation is set apart by a shift toward electric vehicles (EVs) and the improvement of independent vehicles. This change holds the possibility to diminish ozone harming substance emanations and reform metropolitan versatility. Notwithstanding, it accompanies administrative and moral difficulties, for example, guaranteeing the wellbeing of independent vehicles and tending to the effect on conventional transportation occupations. The important point is that transportation is at a junction, and we should adjust the quest for development with the need to address related social and financial ramifications.

The worldwide economy is going through huge changes, driven by globalization, arising economies, and mechanical advancement. As conventional monetary powers face contest from developing business sectors, the important point is that flexibility and advancement will be vital to financial progress from now on. We should embrace change and look for chances to team up on a worldwide scale.

Instruction is developing with the ascent of internet learning and advanced stages. The future will probably see a mix of conventional and computerized learning, customized educational plans, and an emphasis on versatile abilities.

The focal point is that instruction is not generally restricted to the study hall; it is a long lasting excursion of gaining new information and abilities. Embracing computerized training devices and cultivating a culture of interest and nonstop learning are fundamental.

In the domain of legislative issues and worldwide relations, we are confronted with a scope of worldwide difficulties, from psychological oppression to digital fighting. The ascent of populism and dangers to popularity based standards are additionally not too far off. The important point is that worldwide issues request global participation and tact. Our common difficulties require aggregate arrangements, and we should stay focused on maintaining majority rule standards even notwithstanding difficulty.

Pondering the aggregate information and thoughts introduced in this text, a few ongoing ideas become evident. One is the requirement for flexibility and strength despite fast change. What's to come is set apart by vulnerability, yet additionally rich with amazing open doors for those will embrace advancement and ceaseless learning.

Another normal topic is the reliance of our worldwide local area. Whether tending to environmental change, worldwide wellbeing emergencies, or the difficulties of room investigation, the arrangements require joint effort on a global scale. We are partners coming soon for our planet and the advancement of our species, and our activities have broad results.

Moral contemplations are additionally conspicuous. As we push the limits of innovation and science, we should stay careful in maintaining moral standards and guaranteeing that the advantages of progress are open to all, as opposed to fueling disparities.

9.3 Encouraging Local Economies and Small Businesses

In an undeniably globalized world, where global companies and internet business goliaths overwhelm the monetary scene, it is a higher priority than any time in recent memory to perceive and uphold the crucial job that nearby economies and private ventures play in our networks. The flexibility and liveliness of nearby economies are fundamental for financial development as well as for cultivating a feeling of local area, safeguarding social character, and advancing supportability. In this conversation, we will investigate the meaning of nearby economies and private ventures and talk about techniques to support their development and advancement.

Private ventures are much of the time the foundation of nearby economies. They come in different structures, from family-claimed shops and eateries to neighborhood craftsmans and specialist organizations. These undertakings add to monetary development by making position, driving advancement, and infusing cash into the local area. Truth be told, private ventures are much of the time a critical wellspring of work, especially in rustic regions and unassuming communities. They likewise assist with decreasing pay disparity by giving open doors to a different scope of people.

Nearby organizations cultivate a feeling of local area and social character. They are a basic piece of the social texture, where occupants shop as well as accumulate, interface, and fabricate connections. The proprietors and representatives of these organizations are many times dynamic members locally, supporting neighborhood causes and adding to the general prosperity of the area. The recognizable faces and customized administration presented by nearby organizations make a feeling of having a place and trust that is more uncommon in bigger, unoriginal enterprises.

Furthermore, nearby organizations assume a basic part in advancing supportability. They will more often than not source their bits of feedbacks locally, decreasing the carbon impression related with transportation. Supporting nearby farming and assembling can assist with limiting the natural effect of creation and conveyance. Besides, private ventures frequently have a personal stake in the drawn out wellbeing of their local area and are bound to embrace supportable practices that benefit the climate and people in the future.

Empowering nearby economies and independent companies isn't simply a question of wistfulness or local area soul; it is an essential move for financial soundness and strength. Here are a few critical systems to help and advance nearby organizations:

Purchase Nearby: One of the most immediate methods for supporting neighborhood organizations is to put forth a cognizant attempt to purchase from them. Decide to shop at nearby business sectors, eat at neighborhood cafés, and use the administrations of nearby suppliers whenever the situation allows. Thusly, you are guaranteeing that your cash stays inside the local area and adds to its monetary wellbeing.

Advance Mindfulness: Urge your local area to perceive and celebrate nearby organizations. Occasions, for example, "Independent venture Saturday" and neighborhood market fairs can cause to notice the remarkable contributions of nearby undertakings. Furthermore, informal proposals and positive audits on web-based stages can assist with helping the perceivability of private ventures.

Coordinated effort: Independent ventures can profit from cooperation with one another and with neighborhood associations. Joint showcasing endeavors, like cross-advancements or local area occasions, can assist independent ventures with pooling assets and contact a more extensive crowd. Joint efforts can likewise make a feeling of solidarity and common perspective among neighborhood business visionaries.

Monetary Help: Admittance to capital is really difficult for the overwhelming majority independent ventures. State run administrations and monetary foundations can give credits, awards, and monetary schooling to assist entrepreneurs with beginning, extend, or recuperate from misfortunes. By offering low-interest advances or awards designated at independent ventures, state run administrations can animate nearby monetary development.

Work on Guidelines: Over the top or complex guidelines can be an obstruction for private ventures. State run administrations and neighborhood specialists ought to attempt to smooth out guidelines, making it more straightforward for independent ventures to work without being impeded by regulatory obstacles. This incorporates disentangling authorizing and allowing processes.

Give Preparing and Instruction: Entrepreneurs might not approach similar assets and information as huge partnerships. Giving preparation and training on points like computerized showcasing, monetary administration, and maintainable practices can assist private ventures with flourishing in a cutthroat market.

Energize Advancement: Independent companies can be hotbeds of development. Empowering inventiveness and giving assets to innovative work can assist neighborhood organizations with staying cutthroat and adjust to changing business sector elements.

Support Business: Advancing business locally can assist with cultivating a culture of development and financial development. Enterprising training, mentorship projects, and business hatcheries can engage people to begin their own organizations and add to the nearby economy.

Reasonable Practices: Private companies frequently have greater adaptability in taking on economical practices. Empowering them to limit squander, lessen energy utilization, and use eco-accommodating materials can emphatically affect both the climate and the neighborhood local area's picture.

Financial Enhancement: Empowering a different scope of independent companies, from retail and administrations to assembling and innovation, can assist with making a strong nearby economy. Broadening limits the gamble related with over-reliance on a solitary industry or market.

Put resources into Framework: States and neighborhood specialists ought to put resources into foundation that upholds nearby organizations, like open transportation, energetic public spaces, and dependable utilities. A very much kept up with framework can draw in clients and improve the general business climate.

Online Presence: In an undeniably advanced world, private ventures can profit from laying out a web-based presence. This incorporates having a site, involving web-based entertainment for promoting, and partaking in online business stages. A web-based presence can assist independent ventures with arriving at a more extensive client base and adjust to changing purchaser ways of behaving.

www.ingramcontent.com/pod-product-compliance
Lightning Source LLC
LaVergne TN
LVHW051305200726

843510LV00010B/1296